The New Teacher's
Complete Sourcebook

Middle School

BY PAULA NAEGLE

SCHOLASTIC
PROFESSIONAL BOOKS

NEW YORK ● TORONTO ● LONDON ● AUCKLAND ● SYDNEY
MEXICO CITY ● NEW DELHI ● HONG KONG ● BUENOS AIRES

Cover design by James Sarfati
Interior design by Kathy Massaro

ISBN 0-439-30302-8
Copyright © 2002 by Paula Naegle
All rights reserved.
Printed in U.S.A.

1 2 3 4 5 6 7 8 9 10   40   09 08 07 06 05 04 03 02

Contents

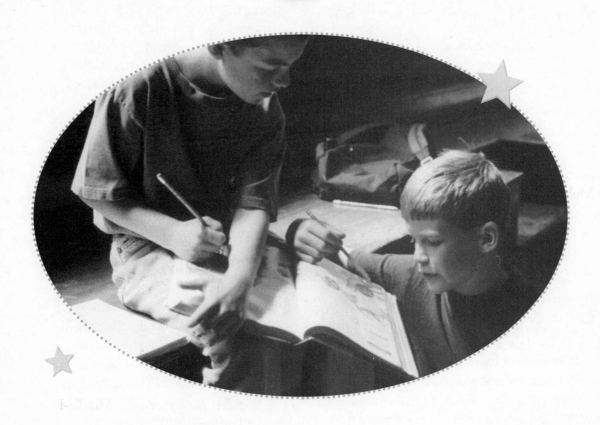

"Help!
I'm going to be
a middle school
teacher!"

Y ou've got the papers that make you official (college degree, teaching license). You have completed your student teaching with flying colors, and you have hundreds of pages that you photocopied from your cooperating teacher's files, so you shouldn't run out of ideas until April. Why are you so nervous?

If you are like many other new teachers who have just received their first assignment to teach middle-level students, you may be feeling a little uneasy. Don't panic. They are just kids—kids "in the middle," who are experiencing more physical and emotional changes than at any other time of their lives!

Teaching middle-level students is an opportunity to hone your classroom management skills and to sharpen your sense of humor. The more organized and prepared you are, the more successful you and your students will be. If you are preparing for the first days of school, then you have time to really think about how you will create an environment that is optimal for learning and is safe and orderly for students who will inhabit that space every day.

Perhaps the most important factor contributing to teacher success is high expectations. As you plan and prepare for your first year of teaching middle school, expect the best. Know that your positive attitude and high hopes for your students will be communicated to them in many ways. From the way that you introduce yourself on the very first day to your celebration of student achievement through positive feedback—your students are watching you to see if you believe in them.

You will make a positive difference in their lives by encouraging them to set goals and then helping them work hard to achieve their dreams. Someday, some of your students will come back to visit you, just to tell you "thanks." Then you will know that you made one of the best career decisions of your life when you accepted a teaching position in middle school. I hope this book—which is filled with insights and practical advice on everything from preparation, procedures and rules, and the classroom environment, to effective lesson plans, motivational methods, assessment and grading, resources, and support—helps you on your journey to becoming a great teacher.

Paula Naegle

CHAPTER 1

Great Beginnings:

Procedures and Routines for Success

What goes into making the classroom environment a friendly, organized, work-centered place where students feel welcome? *Structure.* In fact, structure is key when it comes to planning for a smooth-running classroom. *Middle school students need—and want—structure.* They also need to know what your expectations are if they are to be successful. If you have ever watched an effective teacher, you surely recognize that his or her success in the classroom is not an accident. Effective teachers are PREPARED! And in the classroom, there are many procedures that deserve your careful attention before students arrive.

Procedures tell students how something is to be done. (Procedures are different from *rules*, which are addressed in Chapter 3). Once students understand and are able to carry out procedures correctly, they will eventually do them automatically, without constant prompting. It is the teacher's job to teach, model, and reinforce procedures so that they become *routines* for the students.

Consider some of the following classroom procedures:

- ⚬ Entering the classroom
- ⚬ Beginning class
- ⚬ Dismissal at the end of the period
- ⚬ Transitions between activities
- ⚬ Obtaining supplies and materials
- ⚬ Heading on papers
- ⚬ Turning in homework
- ⚬ Sharpening pencils
- ⚬ Restroom passes
- ⚬ Asking questions
- ⚬ Finishing work early
- ⚬ Passing in papers
- ⚬ Finding make-up work after being absent
- ⚬ Moving into cooperative groups
- ⚬ Fire drills & other emergency procedures

Remember that middle-level students have five other teachers whose procedures may be different from yours. You may want to get together with some of the other middle-level teachers before the start of the school year to agree upon a set of uniform procedures (for those not already regulated by your school district). *Plan on spending a lot of time teaching your classroom procedures, practicing them with your students, and reinforcing them during the first few weeks of school.*

Best Kept Secret

Effective teachers manage their classrooms with procedures—and they prepare! In advance of the first day of school, they have thought about what they want students to do and how these things should be done. When you inform students right from the start how you expect them to behave and work in the classroom, you establish your authority, and they can get down to the serious business of learning.

Teaching Classroom Procedures

It would be so easy if all we had to do was tell our students what all of our classroom procedures are on the first day of school. In a perfect world, they would remember the procedures and follow them without fail until the very last day of school. Dream on! They are kids. They will forget. Make learning the procedures a concrete, hands-on activity throughout the first few weeks of school. Begin with the most important procedures: entering the classroom, opening of class, transitions, and dismissal. Then you may add other procedures later (i.e., heading on papers, turning in homework, sharpening pencils, etc.).

In his book, *The First Days of School: How to Be an Effective Teacher*, Dr. Harry Wong suggests a three-step process for teaching classroom procedures to students:

STEP 1: *Explain Classroom Procedures Clearly*

Effective teachers know what activities need to be done and have worked out the procedures for each of them. These procedures are posted or distributed to the students early in the school year or when the activity surfaces in class.

Explain

- ✧ Define the procedure in concrete terms.

- ✧ Demonstrate the procedure; don't just tell.

- ✧ Demonstrate a complex procedure step by step.

STEP 2: *Rehearse Classroom Procedures Until They Become Routines*

Effective teachers spend a good deal of time during the first weeks of school introducing, teaching, modeling, and rehearsing procedures. Watch a good music, drama, athletic, or foreign-language coach. Such people are masters at the rehearsal technique. They tell and show you a technique, even have you watch a video of the technique. Then they have you do it repeatedly while they watch you. Some people call this technique "guided practice."

Tip

Post your procedures in a prominent place. This is a good way to remind students of how things are to be done in your classroom. See the sample procedures chart on page 12.

STEP 3: *Reinforce a Correct Procedure and Reteach an Incorrect One*

☼ Determine whether students have learned the procedure or whether they need further explanation, demonstration, or practice.

☼ Reteach the correct procedure if the rehearsal is unacceptable, and give corrective feedback.

☼ Praise the students when the rehearsal is acceptable.

Reprinted with permission of the author, Dr. Harry Wong. *The First Days of School: How to be an Effective Teacher*, by Harry K. Wong and Rosemary Tripi Wong. Harry Wong Publications, 1991.

Sign outside of teacher's door to remind students about the procedure for entering the classroom when tardy ▶

IF YOU ARE TARDY TO CLASS...

1. ENTER CLASS <u>QUIETLY</u>.

2. SIGN THE <u>TARDY LOG</u>.

3. PROCEED <u>QUIETLY</u> TO YOUR SEAT AND <u>JOIN IN THE LESSON</u>.

THANK YOU

The First Five Minutes

The first five minutes of the class period are golden. Since people tend to remember best what happens first and last, these first few minutes are "prime time" for learning. To maximize the effective use of class time, taking attendance should wait until after the students are engaged in a learning activity. For some teachers, the opening activity is a routine that is the same every day; for other teachers, it is the "launch" for a lesson. The following are sample routines for the first five minutes of class:

- ✲ Problem of the day

- ✲ Journal writing

- ✲ Terra Nova sample test question

- ✲ Brain teaser requiring critical thinking

- ✲ Vocabulary "Word of the Day"

- ✲ React to a quotation

- ✲ Warm-up problem on overhead to copy and solve

- ✲ Watch video news clip of a current event or topic related to course content

- ✲ Respond to a newspaper editorial

- ✲ Conundrum (Students tackle a puzzling question or problem. They may ask the teacher yes or no questions to try to arrive at an answer. For example: *What occurs once in a minute, twice in a moment, but never in a thousand years?* Answer: *The letter* m.)

- ✲ Daily Oral Language, Math, etc.

- ✲ Creative Questions (Teacher supplies the answer first, then students generate questions that will fit the answer. For example, if the answer is *zero*, possible questions might include, *What number multiplied by itself will always equal itself?* or *What is a word that rhymes with hero?*)

Classroom Procedures

I. When the tardy bell rings...

1. Be in your seat ready to work quietly.

2. Place your homework assignment on your desk so it is ready to be collected.

3. Begin the Opening Activity: directions are on the overhead each day.

4. Wait quietly for the teacher's instruction.

II. To obtain the teacher's attention...

ONE FINGER = I need to sharpen my pencil.
TWO FINGERS = I need a tissue.
THREE FINGERS = I need your help.

III. When you see the teacher's hand signal...

1. Freeze (stop what you are doing).

2. Gently tap on your neighbor's arm to get his/her attention to freeze.

3. Face the teacher and listen to instructions.

IV. When the dismissal bell rings...

1. At the sound of the bell, close your book and stop working.

2. Stay in your seat until you hear the teacher dismiss you.

3. Leave quietly and in an orderly manner.

V. If you choose to break a rule...

1st Time = Verbal warning
2nd Time = Parent contact (phone, e-mail, or card sent home)
3rd Time = Teacher detention
4th Time = Counselor referral
5th Time = Dean referral

The New Teacher's Complete Sourcebook: Middle School   Scholastic Professional Books

The best opening activities are those that get kids to settle down and focus on an academic task related to your curriculum. In my class, I explain to students that they will earn "participation points" for completing the daily opening activity. However, if students see this activity as busywork, then they may use the time to fool around. When you relate the opening activity to the lesson, students will see the connection and be more inclined to participate each day.

Remember, you set the tone for the class period every day during the first five minutes. Teach students the procedure for beginning your class. Reinforce the procedure by expecting students to follow it, practicing it the first week of school, and reinforcing it each day. After a while, this procedure should become a routine that makes your "beginning of class" run smoothly.

Experienced Teachers Share Their Beginning-of-Class Routines

The first few minutes are crucial. Students must know what they are expected to do as soon as the tardy bell rings. **I do not allow "free time"** while I take roll. My students learn during the first week to be in their seats **ready** to work when the bell rings. I assign a monitor to turn on the overhead, where the Opening Activity is for students to do while I take roll. The monitor then distributes work to be done or assignments that have been graded. Students returning from an absence use this time to write down work missed (from the Make-Up Notebook).

—*Patricia Revzin, English teacher*

As students file in, I remind them of the materials they will need that day, and to have pencils sharpened and paper out. Then, the minute the bell rings, I turn on the overhead projector to reveal a warm-up problem. The problem is either a review of a recent lesson or of important information I don't want the students to forget, such as basic math skills. As they are working on the problem, I take roll and walk around the room to check students' progress and answer quick questions. When students have finished the warm-up, we either go over it as a class or it is treated as a quiz and is collected to be graded.

—*Eric Johnson, math teacher*

*“*The first five minutes of class are devoted to either a preview or review activity. The format of the activity varies. Students might be asked to write a reaction to a quotation or newspaper article, copy a time line, brainstorm emotions felt in response to a piece of music, or take a quiz on the previous night's reading assignment. Whatever the opening activity, its primary purpose is to engage students the minute they walk through the door and to give me an opportunity to handle attendance and other housekeeping duties. The opening activity also provides a jumping-off point for the day's lesson.*”*

—*Heidi Olive, social studies teacher*

Getting Your Students' Attention

There may be several times during a class period when it becomes necessary for you to get the attention of your students in order to facilitate a transition. Sometimes they will be working in small groups— which requires talking and possibly movement throughout the classroom. Avoid the new teacher trap of raising your voice to get their attention. Educational research indicates that the louder the teacher's voice, the louder the students' voices will be. Instead of shouting, establish a procedure for quieting the class so that you can give them further instructions and transition to the next activity. Here are some effective signals used by new and experienced teachers:

- ☼ Chimes, bell, or rain stick

- ☼ Holding up a hand (All students raise their hands and close their mouths when they see you hold up your hand.)

- ☼ "Clap once when you hear my voice." (Clap) "Clap twice when you hear my voice." (Clap, Clap) "Clap three times when you hear my voice." (Clap, Clap, Clap)

- ☼ 5, 4, 3, 2, 1 Countdown (Teach students the steps for each of the numbers):

  - ◆ 5: Freeze
  - ◆ 4: Quiet
  - ◆ 3: Eyes on the teacher
  - ◆ 2: Hands free (put things down)
  - ◆ 1: Listen for instructions

If none of these signals appeal to you, talk to other teachers in your building to find out how they get the attention of their students. The trick is to find one that fits your personality—and that works! Remember that you must explain the new procedure, practice it with your students, and consistently reinforce the signal if you want your students to adopt it as a routine. Try to use the signal frequently during the first weeks of school and explain that you are timing them to see how quickly they respond to the signal. You can even make it a contest to see which class period can respond the most quickly to your signal.

Dismissal Procedures

The way that you dismiss students will have an impact on their behavior in the hallways and possibly their behavior in the next class. If you maximize the minutes of your class period, students will be working up until the bell rings. Plan to teach from bell to bell, and you will avoid the down time that inevitably leads to students misbehaving for lack of something productive to do. On the very first day of school, explain to your students that you have a procedure for dismissing them.

> Students, we will be working throughout the entire period of this class each day. We won't pack up and get ready to leave five minutes before the bell rings. Instead, we will pause after the bell rings to make sure that all the garbage is picked up off the floor. Please look around you to see that the area around your desk is clean and that materials are put away. Then when we are ready, you will hear me say the magic words: "Thank you, and have a great day!" Those words are what will dismiss you to leave the room. The bell does not dismiss you, I do. Let's practice...

Of course, just because you explained the dismissal procedure, modeled it for the students, and practiced it with them, does not mean that they will remember what to do on the first day...or the second. If they begin to pack up before the end of the period, stop and remind them, "Students, we have a procedure for dismissing class each day. Who can tell me what that procedure is?" Remind students how you will dismiss them. After the first few days, they will remember what to do. **BE CONSISTENT!** If you stop using the procedure, students will quickly forget, and they will begin to put away materials and line up at the door before the bell rings.

Attendance Procedures

Attendance must be checked carefully, in accordance with your school district's regulations, and be reported accurately to the office. In most districts, the responsibility for taking attendance *must not be delegated to a student*, so check with your administrator for the policies and procedures required for taking attendance.

While the matter of taking attendance is very important, it can be done very quickly with minimum disruption to the teaching/learning process. Below are some tips on establishing a procedure for taking attendance.

☼ **Get students engaged in the lesson.** Establish a routine for your students to do at the beginning of each period such as journal writing, daily oral math (DOM), or copying the daily objective in their student planners. As students are quietly working, you will be free to take attendance.

☼ **Use a seating chart.** Write students' names in pencil so that if you need to make changes, you do not have to recreate the chart. Some teachers use 2- by 1-inch Post-it® notes for students' names on the seating chart so it is easy to make changes when necessary. Place your seating chart in a clear page protector, so you can use an overhead pen or washable marker to mark absences and tardies on the seating chart when you take attendance. It is much faster than trying to read your attendance roster and look around to see that each student is present. Then, once students are engaged in a learning activity, you can mark the attendance sheets for the office and your attendance book. The page protector can be wiped clean for the next day.

☼ **Use correct attendance symbols.** For purposes of uniformity, most school districts require teachers to use certain symbols to document attendance. Check with your supervising administrator for advice on how to document students' absences and mark attendance accordingly in your permanent record book.

Assigning Seats
and Using Seating Charts

Welcome students to your room when they arrive on the first day—and assign them a seat. If you have your class roster in advance, this task is fairly easy to do. Label the rows A, B, C, D, etc., and then number the seats from front to back. If your seating arrangement utilizes tables or groups of desks, you may label the groups accordingly. (See sample seating arrangements Chapter 2.) You can also assign seats to students randomly as they arrive, even if you don't have the roster in advance. As students enter, greet them at the door, jot their names on the chart, and direct them to their seats.

A 1	B 1	C 1	D 1	E 1	F 1
John A.	Jennifer E.		Jessica N.		Rachel W.
A 2	**B 2**	**C 2**	**D 2**	**E 2**	**F 2**
Megan B.	Brad G.	Julie Ann K.	Whitney O.	Blanca S.	
A 3	**B 3**	**C 3**	**D 3**	**E 3**	**F 3**
Chris B.	Emily H.	Trent L.	Jonathan P.	Ross S.	Sandra W.
A 4	**B 4**	**C 4**	**D 4**	**E 4**	**F 4**
Pete C.	Ryan J.	Kenny M.	Bryana P.	Russell T.	Charley Y.
A 5	**B 5**	**C 5**	**D 5**	**E 5**	**F 5**
Susan D.	Melina J.	Sara M.	Natalie R.	Crystal U.	

You may choose to wait until the second day (or later) to assign seats, so you can put students in alphabetical order and reserve certain seats for students who need to be close to the front of the room for visual or auditory reasons. Make sure that you inform your students on the first day that they will be having assigned seating starting the next day. When assigning places, make sure to assign them before the students get seated. It is much easier to seat students in their assigned places before class begins rather than having them get comfortable, and then moving them later during the period. There is also less grumbling and resistance if you point out their new seats when they enter the classroom.

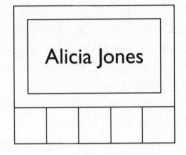

> I create a seating chart on the computer that matches the setup of my classroom. It consists of a square of each student's name with five small boxes attached, one for each day of the week (see figure at right). I then place the seating chart in a **plastic sheet protector**. This allows me to use **an overhead marker** to take attendance quickly by marking an 'X' in the corresponding box of each student who is absent. Tardies are noted with a 'T.' The five boxes also give me a quick idea of how many days any particular student was absent and/or tardy that week. I also include some points of reference to help substitute teachers determine how to read the seating chart. Marking the 'front' of the room or showing where the teacher desk is placed is helpful.

—*Eric Johnson, math teacher*

Absences and Make-Up Work

Keeping track of missing assignments when students have been absent can be a horrendous task if you do not have a system in place from the beginning of the school year. It is important for students to take responsibility for obtaining work that was missed during an absence. Otherwise, you may find yourself going crazy trying to track down students who have incomplete assignments. Keep your sanity and your good humor by requiring students to consult the class Make-Up Calendar or Folder, which you store in a convenient spot in the classroom. Consider posting a large sign directly above the make-up folder (see right).

Often when students return to school after being absent, they are concerned about what they have missed. You may not have enough time to tell each individual absentee all of the pertinent details from the previous day's lesson, so put a procedure in place for students to

Make it easy for your students to locate any assignments they may have missed when they were absent. ▶

collect their make-up work quickly and efficiently. Either you or a designated student can write down the necessary work to be completed at the end of each period. Extra copies of handouts and/or worksheets can be dated and placed in the make-up folder for students to pick up when they return to school after being absent.

Encourage students to find a "Homework Buddy" with whom they can exchange telephone numbers. Then, if a student misses a lecture or class in which notes were to be taken, he can get a copy of the notes from a homework buddy. Also, the homework buddy can clarify any questions regarding projects or assignments given when a student was absent.

Establish "Office Hours." Designate a certain time that you are always available for students to make up quizzes and tests or get extra help, such as Wednesdays after school. Be consistent, so that students know they can make appointments to get caught up with tests they have missed. Remember to state your make-up policy in your course expectations so students and parents are clearly aware of your procedures. Here is a sample blurb from course expectations by Casey Robbins, a language arts teacher:

Make-Up Work Policy

After you are absent, you should consult the class make-up assignment notebook for the class activities, assignments, and handouts that you missed. Once you complete this process, I will be happy to help you with any questions that you have. Work that was assigned before you were absent should be ready to be turned in upon arrival back to school. You will be given two days to make up any work that was assigned when you were absent. If you know in advance that you will have an extended absence, please arrange to collect the work beforehand.

You may want to design a form for students to attach to their make-up work so that you know exactly what you are grading when the student turns it in. The following example is from Sandy Ginger's science class.

* Tip *

You can purchase a ream of two-copy no carbon required (NCR) paper from most office supply stores for students to use when taking notes for an absent homework buddy. The NCR paper is more convenient for students who may not have access to a photocopy machine, and there is less chance of the notes getting lost. This strategy can also be used as an accommodation for special needs students who require written notes from the class lectures.

Make-Up Work

Name: _____ **Period:** _____

Return Date: _____

☼ *There is a copy of notes we took in the sample notebook (you can do during class today).*

☼ *Tests, labs, and quizzes must be made up after school within one week of your return.*

☼ *No credit for copying.*

Absent on: _____ **Absence #:** _____

1. Assignment(s) due the day you were gone:

_____

_____

_____

This is due NOW or late penalties apply.

2. Assignments you missed: These are due:

_____   _____

_____   _____

_____   _____

_____   _____

_____   _____

PLEASE TURN THIS FORM IN WITH YOUR MAKE-UP WORK!

The New Teacher's Complete Sourcebook: Middle School   Scholastic Professional Books

Helping New Students Feel Welcome—And Up to Speed

It would be easy if the students that we have on the first day of school remained in our classes until the very end of the year. However, the reality is that there will probably be students entering and withdrawing from your classroom throughout the year. How do you help a new student make the transition into your classroom smoothly? First of all, be prepared with a folder containing pertinent information that she can read while you get the class going on an assignment. You will not have time to stop your class and spend 45 minutes talking with that individual, but you can have materials ready for her that will explain your classroom rules and expectations. Then you can follow up with a one-on-one conversation before the end of the period.

You may want to put together a "Guide to Success in Our Class" notebook, containing information that you and your students have contributed. It should contain an explanation about the behavior expected during small-group work and important procedures such as: "What to Do When You Have Been Absent," and "How to Get Help on Assignments." New students can read the guidebook on their first day, and then return it to you before the end of the period. You may want to prepare a scavenger hunt or some other activity so your new student will have to look for key items such as the title of the textbook you're using or restroom passes, while browsing through the guidebook. Consider including a page or two written by some of your students, entitled "How to Get a Good Grade in Ms. Smith's English Class."

Assign your new student a class "buddy" to help her become familiar with the procedures in your classroom. Seat the new student near the assigned "buddy," so that she can ask questions if necessary. Potential "buddies" are students who are naturally friendly and enjoy being helpful. Let your students know at the beginning of the year that you may be asking for their assistance when new students join your class later in the year. You might suggest that the "buddy" eat lunch with the new student on this first day. Almost everyone knows what it feels like to be new, so most students are willing to take on the role of being a "buddy" for the first week. You can reward the "buddy" by giving him/her a free homework pass or a special privilege for being helpful.

The important thing to remember is that a new student needs and deserves the same attention and respect that you give all of your students on the first day of school. Help new students feel welcome by being prepared for their arrival. Make it a point to learn their names the first day and then check in with them before and after class each day during that first week to see how they are doing. They will be very grateful for your kindness and attention.

❋ Tip ❋

A new student folder should contain the following:

- ❖ Course expectations
- ❖ Information for parents
- ❖ Journal topic: *Please tell me about yourself.*
- ❖ Student interest inventory
- ❖ Pretest (to assess entry-level knowledge and skills)
- ❖ Textbook check-out card

You Don't Need
to Spend
a Fortune:

Preparing Your Classroom

My first classroom was approximately the size of a closet and was stuffed with student desks, a large teacher's desk, and one filing cabinet. When I first saw it, I felt overwhelmed and a little depressed. The room was dull, drab, and uninviting. How could I inspire students to want to learn in such an unappealing environment? With a little creativity and a lot of hard work, I transformed that room into a "home away from home." Students need to feel welcome, and your classroom environment will convey an impression of warmth and comfort if you take the time to prepare it well in advance of their arrival.

Setting Up Your Classroom

Preparing your classroom for the arrival of your students is probably high on your list of priorities—and should be. A welcoming environment can set the stage for learning, but before you go out and spend a fortune on commercial posters, take the time to think about the basics. Remember that decorating the classroom is the frosting on the cake.

The physical layout of your classroom will determine the flow of traffic and ease of movement for you and your students. Even if your classroom is small, you have a lot of choices when it comes to arranging students' desks. The room arrangement should match your purpose for the lesson. If you are planning direct instruction or a lecture format, then rows of desks facing the teacher and white board or screen is your best bet. When all desks are facing the front of the room, student attention is more likely to be focused on the presenter—you.

For small group work, students can be shown how to transform their rows into clusters of four or five by moving their desks into small groups. If you begin the year with students facing each other in small groups, you can expect that students will get the message that it is okay to talk to each other. However, it may be wise to begin the year with the students' attention focused on you, since you need their undivided attention while you teach them your procedures and expectations. There will be time for creative grouping later.

Carefully consider where you will place the following items:

- ☼ **Overhead projector and screen** All your students must be able to see the screen without having to crane their necks. Try sitting in different students' seats to find out if you can see the board.

- ☼ **Pencil sharpener and trash can** Place them so they are not directly next to student desks to avoid constant disruptions during class.

- ☼ **Supplies and materials** If you frequently use supplementary textbooks or other materials that students must obtain during class, keep them in an accessible area. Items that are only used occasionally can be stored in a cabinet.

- ☼ **Teacher's desk** If it is tucked away from the main traffic flow of your room, it will be less tempting for students to touch or remove items that are off limits.

- ☼ **Students' desks** Do you want your students to face the door? You may not have a choice, but consider the interruptions that can occur during a typical class period. If possible, you may want to orient the class away from the door. Since you need to be mobile, constantly moving throughout the classroom to monitor student progress, leave walkway space between rows and especially at the back of your classroom. See diagrams on the next page.

Sample Seating Arrangements

Unless your chairs and desks are bolted to the floor, you will have flexibility in how you arrange the seating in your classroom. Match the seating arrangement with the format and activities of your lesson plan. Be creative!

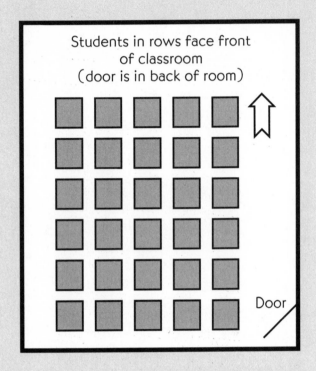

Students in rows face front of classroom (door is in back of room)

Door

1

Traditional rows in columns are ideal for establishing classroom management. This arrangement allows students to focus on you when you are lecturing or teaching routines and procedures. It is great for **direct instruction**.

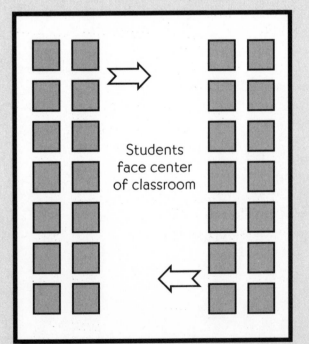

Students face center of classroom

2

Position student desks so that they **face the center** when you are facilitating **classroom discussions**. The outer area is ideal for **skits, role playing, and student demonstrations**. It creates a friendlier atmosphere and can be used in lieu of traditional rows.

Sample Seating Arrangements (Continued)

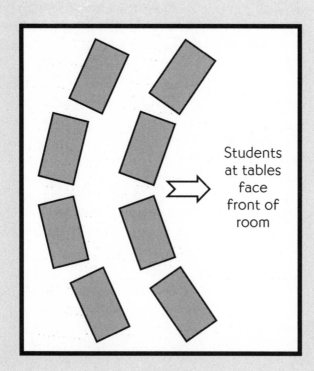

Students at tables face front of room

3

Situate chairs around tables so that **students do not have their backs facing you**. When it is time for small group activities, they can move their chairs to face each other. This arrangement is ideal for **cooperative learning activities**. Be aware that seating students in groups invites dialogue, which is great if that is your purpose.

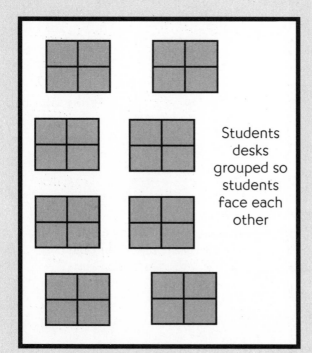

Students desks grouped so students face each other

4

This format is wonderful if you have desks because you can rearrange them from traditional rows into groups and back again, depending on your lesson plan. **Teach students how to quickly rearrange the desks to facilitate small group work.**

Enhancing Your Classroom Environment

First impressions last! When your students enter the classroom on the first day, what impression do you want them to have? Obviously, a positive one. However, even if you don't have a generous budget at your disposal, you can create an inviting atmosphere by using some fairly simple, inexpensive materials. Most schools provide wide butcher paper in bold colors that you can use to cover bulletin boards. My first classroom (which was the size of a closet) had no bulletin boards, so I improvised by covering several large (10- by 5-foot) areas with butcher paper and scalloped borders. I updated the "boards" every month to reflect current topics that we were covering. Take pictures of your bulletin boards so you can remember themes that worked well and make improvements in future years.

Some secondary teachers think that attractive bulletin boards are not necessary on the middle-school level. According to Eric Jensen, author of *Brain-Based Learning*, "90% of the brain's sensory input is from visual sources" and "the brain has an immediate and primitive response to symbols, icons and strong, simple images." If you want to connect with your visual learners, then utilize more visuals such as colorful posters, mind maps, vivid drawings, and symbols to capture their attention.

There should also be variety to your bulletin boards. The information and decoration can change throughout the year to reflect curriculum content and seasonal themes. It's also helpful to designate one bulletin board in a centrally located area of your classroom for important school information. Many students do not hear the daily announcements, so when they ask you questions about upcoming activities, you can direct them to the daily bulletin posted on the information board. Keep this board current throughout the year.

School Matters

Items to post on a "School Matters" bulletin board:

- Fire drill map
- Tardy policy
- Activities calendar
- Absence policy
- Daily announcements
- Assembly bell schedule
- School dress code
- Classroom rules
- Make-up work policy
- School mission

☀ Tip ☀

66 A colorfully decorated bulletin board makes the classroom more inviting for students and the instructor. I find the brightest color paper I can find (such as the non-fade fuchsia available at most teaching supply stores) and then accent the board with a contrasting border. I like to create a 'passageway' based on a theme. I tell my students, 'My door is the passageway; what you learn in my class will take you somewhere when you leave.' **99**

—Heidi Olive, social studies teacher

Inexpensive Ways to Decorate Your Classroom Walls

☼ **Use old calendars with great pictures.** Tell your friends and family members that you need their old calendars. Laminate the pictures and you will have a collection of visuals with a theme. Be on the lookout for great calendars when you travel, especially in the summer when the current year's calendars are selling for half price.

☼ **Ask for movie posters that theaters are discarding.** If you smile and explain that you are an educator, that your students "would absolutely LOVE to have that poster in the classroom," you would be surprised how willing businesses are to contribute to your cause.

☼ **Do a colorful and visually attractive project with your students during the first week of school, then display the work on your walls.** If you cannot tie the first class project in with your curriculum, consider an autobiographical project wherein students use pictures and symbols to represent themselves. A project such as this allows students to get acquainted and feel as though they are contributing members of the learning community.

☼ **Design a mystery board that presents a problem or concept from the curriculum that you teach.** Pique students' interest by posing a question or using terminology to be learned during the semester. Make the mystery relevant and intriguing.

☼ **Put up quotations by famous mathematicians or athletes.** Use their words to inspire students to higher levels of achievement. You can print them on a banner using your computer, or use stencils.

☼ **Create borders for your bulletin board using newspaper.** Cut newspaper into a 4-inch wide strip and scallop one side.

✧ **Display postcards or other memorabilia from places where you have traveled.** You may even number the postcards and see if students can guess where they are from.

✧ **Use comic strips and/or political cartoons related to your curriculum.** You can enlarge them on the photocopier and laminate the copies. (Newsprint sometimes turns yellow and creases when you laminate it.)

To introduce yourself to students, create a bulletin board featuring your interests, hobbies, and family.

✧ **Display newspaper editorials pertaining to your curriculum.** This will encourage students to think critically about controversial issues related to the content of your course.

✧ **Involve students in creating a collage using a collection of interesting objects, such as book jackets or CD covers.** It may seem a little wacky, but remember that the more whimsical, the better. Visit theme restaurants such as Red Robin, Planet Hollywood, or Hard Rock Café for ideas. Your classroom can become a living museum when you tie these artifacts in with your curriculum.

Students created math collages to decorate a bulletin board entitled "Math Rocks Our World." ▶

✧ **Never pass up a garage sale!** You would be amazed at what treasures you will find for your classroom. You may find framed posters as well as items for a prop box to be used when students create skits for vocabulary words.

☼ **Ask travel agencies, local chambers of commerce, National Geographic, and AAA for free maps and posters.** Often they are willing to give away free promotional items.

This gigantic map covers an entire wall in a geography classroom. The clocks identify time zones.

☼ **Cultivate business partnerships.** Link your classroom with a business in the community that is relevant to your curriculum. Introduce yourself with a telephone call and follow-up visit. You will find wonderful resources to enhance your classroom and curriculum. Invite the business partner to be a guest speaker, and then follow up with student-generated thank-you letters. (But be sure to proofread all student letters before you mail them!)

☼ **Create and display posters that illustrate, outline, and reinforce your curriculum.** (Examples: parts of speech, study skills, reading themes, mathematical operations, steps of the writing process, the scientific method of problem solving, periodic table, or historical time lines.)

☼ **Ask other teachers for their cast-offs.** Many experienced teachers have a closet full of old posters that they are tired of using and would be glad to loan (or give) to you. Make sure that you know in advance whether or not they want the items to be returned.

☼ **Remember: Sometimes less is more!** Color is important. Balance is important. But don't overdo it with so many posters and quotations that your environment overwhelms and distracts your students. Keep it simple, colorful, and interesting.

▲

An ambitious reading teacher collected book jackets from young adult fiction and displayed them in a snake design stretching around the perimeter of her classroom.

✳ Tip ✳

❝ I used to cover the walls before students arrived at school, but I don't anymore. I do a colorful and visually attractive project with my students some time in the first week and a half of school, and quickly put the work up on the walls. Students enjoy seeing their projects displayed in the classroom. Remember to change displays about once a month depending on what you are teaching at the time. I usually assign wall stapling and staple removal duties to students who are serving detention, and I make a point of thanking them and praising them for their sense of design, so they feel useful instead of merely punished. I find that this helps me to develop a stronger relationship with those students who need 'extra understanding.' It also saves me a lot of time. ❞

—*Victoria Yeomanson, English Teacher*

Post Learning Objectives and Daily Agenda

If you do not post your daily agenda, you will soon find students asking you, "What are we going to do today?" It won't be just one student, it will be lots of them, and they will ask you that question every period, every day, for the entire school year. Students want to know what to expect, so if you want them to be ready for the activities and procedures in your lesson, list them on the board in the same spot every day.

Language Arts Agenda: September 5, 2001

1 **Journal Writing:** List all of the big and little decisions that you have made in the last twenty-four hours.

2 **Complete Story Map**

3 **Discussion:** Conflict in *The Lady and the Tiger*

4 **Brainstorm Ideas for Essay:** "A Tough Decision"

5 **Homework:** Rough draft of opening paragraph

Advice for Roving Teachers

In some school districts, the number of middle-level students is increasing so quickly that schools are at capacity or beyond. If you are in a school where there are not enough classrooms for each teacher, you may be required to "rove" from classroom to classroom, utilizing the rooms of teachers during their preparation periods. It is not the easiest way to begin your teaching career, but it is possible to be successful in creating a climate conducive to learning, even under such difficult circumstances.

Communication with the teachers whose rooms you will use is very important. Introduce yourself and explain that you are hoping to establish a positive working relationship with each of the teachers. Many teachers have limited budgets (or have to use their own funds) to purchase supplies and decoratives for their classroom, and it is important that other teachers who share this space be respectful of that fact. Ask the teachers to tell you what their concerns are and establish boundaries for using supplies, bulletin boards, textbooks, and other items. Keep the lines of communication open throughout the school year to avoid frustrations and hurt feelings over situations that may arise. Keep your sense of humor. You won't always be a nomadic teacher!

Organization will be the key to your success in staying sane. Even though it is difficult to share classrooms with other teachers, if you are prepared and flexible, you can manage to utilize the learning space effectively.

Tips from Experienced Teachers Who Have Taught from a Cart

✻ Establish an efficient procedure for the beginning of class. Require that students are in their seats before the bell rings and ready to work with the required materials. Teach students that they should *look at the overhead screen to find the opening assignment before the bell rings*, since you probably will not have time to write these instructions on the board before class. That way you can quickly and quietly take attendance using the seating chart while they are engaged in the learning activity. Remember, students want structure!

✻ Provide a two or three minute "Opportunity Period" every day during class (while students are working) so students may ask questions or mention concerns to you. This time for one-on-one contact with students is critical. Some students would rather give up or not ask than try to find you somewhere on campus before or after school.

☼ Request that students who need extra help or need to make up work come to see you before or after school in a *designated classroom*. Reassure them that you want to help them, but since you need to be on your way to the next classroom at the end of each class period, they will have to make use of these specially designated times for extra help.

☼ Negotiate with the regular classroom teacher for a bulletin board to display your students' work and a filing cabinet drawer to store items that you use daily.

Checklist: Preparing for the First Day of School

Use the following checklist before the first day of school. There are so many details to think about that the more things you take care of before school begins, the more relaxed and comfortable you will feel. Show this checklist to your mentor or supervising administrator to see if they can think of other things you'll need to do before the first day.

When you check off the final item, breathe a sigh of relief and know that you've done everything you need to prepare for your debut as a teacher!

Before School Begins

☼ **Become familiar with the school building by locating the following places:**

—— supervising administrator's office

—— principal's secretary

—— fire drill exit route

—— teachers' mailboxes

—— faculty restrooms

—— students' restrooms

—— department coordinator's room

—— department textbook storage area

—— library and technology center (Internet access)

—— audio-visual equipment and supplies

—— photocopier and fax machine

—— graphic arts department

—— counselors' office

—— deans' office

☼ **Obtain basic supplies for your classroom.**

—— first-aid kit	—— paper	—— paper clips
—— tissues	—— pens, pencils	—— file folders
—— stapler, staples	—— chalk, eraser	—— calendar
—— scissors	—— dry-erase markers	—— transparencies
—— overhead markers	—— sticky notes	—— masking tape

(continued on next page)

Before School Begins
(continued)

☼ **Obtain necessary forms from the office.**

—— corridor passes

—— health office passes

—— discipline referrals

—— counselor referrals

—— parent communication cards

☼ **Obtain textbooks for students and locate teacher's manuals.**

☼ **Obtain necessary audio-visual equipment, such as overhead projector, TV, VCR, etc.**

☼ Once you know where things are located and you have obtained supplies, textbooks, and equipment, **prepare your classroom for the first day:**

—— Arrange students' desks/tables in desired pattern.

—— Create an inviting atmosphere—bulletin boards, posters, banners, and calendar.

—— Check to make sure that you have a pencil sharpener, wastebasket, clock, and flag in your classroom.

—— Post your classroom rules and procedures.

—— Know your school's rules, discipline plan, and policies.

—— If possible, have your class roster readily available.

—— Complete the first day's lesson plan and have all materials ready.

—— Prepare first week's lesson plan.

—— Obtain a supply of student information cards (schools sometimes provide these, or you can create your own).

—— Write your name, course title, and class schedule on the board.

The New Teacher's Complete Sourcebook: Middle School   Scholastic Professional Books

CHAPTER 3

No One Slept Well Last Night:

The First Days of School

Don't be surprised if you don't sleep well the night before the first day of school. Your students probably didn't sleep well either. (We won't even mention the insomnia that the principal, assistant principals, school nurse, counselors, and librarian experience!) Even if you are extremely well prepared, you may still wonder if you've thought of everything or if the students will recognize that you are a brand new teacher. Just remember that it is very natural to feel butterflies in your stomach; in fact, many experienced teachers have that same feeling every year on the first day.

What do you need to know to help you make a positive impact on your students from the very first minute? Research on students' responses to meeting a new teacher suggests that you have about *seven seconds to make a first impression* (Robert L. DeBruyn, "Of the First Day," *The Master Teacher*, 1996). "How can that be?" you may wonder. If you only have seven seconds, then the information that students are taking in must be far more than the words you speak. While important, the first thing you say pales in comparison to all of the nonverbal messages that you will convey. Think about the following cues that you telegraph when you first meet your students:

- ✷ Facial expression

- ✷ Posture and body language

- ✷ Clothing

- ✷ Proximity to students

- ✷ Movement in the classroom

- ✷ Volume, pitch, and tone of voice

- ✷ Gestures

- ✷ Room environment

First impressions stick! After the first minute, students are processing everything they observe you do and hear you say by fitting this new information into their initial impression of you. What are students thinking? Here are some possibilities:

- ✷ "She seems nice and fair."

- ✷ "He's going to be strict, but he seems to know what he is doing."

- ✷ "She's nervous and uncertain."

- ✷ "He's yelling at us, but we haven't even done anything wrong yet."

- ✷ "She's mean, and I think this is going to be a bad class."

- ✷ "He likes being a teacher, and he's funny."

Even though you won't know what they are thinking, you can bet that they are forming an opinion of you and your class on the very first day. You must plan what you do and say in advance if you want to create a positive first impression. Happily, you have lots of time to think about those first seven seconds!

Ten Things You Can Do to Create a Positive First Impression:

☼ **Dress for success.** Students notice what you are wearing. In fact, very few details escape their hypercritical eyes. If you have a run in your stockings or a broken fingernail, a middle-school student will probably notice. (Make a point to downplay all personal comments.) You don't have to buy expensive designer clothing to make a good impression, but you do need to dress more formally than your students do. Be neat, clean, pressed, and tucked-in! Wear comfortable shoes. If your feet hurt, and they will on the first day, you may not feel like moving around the classroom much. You will need to be mobile and comfortable, so choose your shoes carefully.

☼ **Meet them at the door.** Welcome your students as they enter the classroom to show them that you are prepared and ready for them to enter. Say "Good morning," or "Good afternoon," as they enter. They may not answer you, but they will recognize that you are being polite and respectful. Not all adults treat adolescents respectfully, so the fact that you have done so will put them at ease and begin to build a relationship of trust.

☼ **Smile.** If someone in your teacher preparation program told you, "Don't smile until Thanksgiving," then you were given bad advice. Greet your students with a warm smile. The smile shows that you are comfortable with your role as a teacher and that you want them to feel comfortable in your classroom.

☼ **Direct students to their assigned seat.** You may think that it is too early to assign seats, but students want to know what to do and where to go when they arrive at a new classroom. If you have your class roster in advance, then this process is easy. You may put a transparency on the overhead projector with a diagram of the seating arrangement or simply put their names on their seats. If you do not know who will be coming to your classroom, you may assign seats easily by giving students a card when they enter which shows their seat number. (Number your desks in advance.) If you plan to assign seating after this first day, remember to inform your students that you will be assigning seats, and then do so the next day.

☼ **Begin immediately after the bell rings.** Again, you will convey that you are prepared and eager to begin the journey that you will take together during the school year. Speak clearly and confidently as you begin, "Good morning ladies and gentlemen. My name is Ms. Naegle, and you are in 7th Grade English, Room 702. Please check your schedule to make sure that you are in the right room."

☼ **Show you care.** Keep your introduction about yourself very brief. Maintain your focus on your students. Young adolescents, on the first day of school, want to know what they are supposed to do. They do not need to know every little detail about your background; and frankly, they don't care on the first day! Middle school students want to know that you care about them. They will care about you after they get to know you and realize that you are organized, capable, and focused on providing high quality instruction. Save your stories about why you decided to become a teacher for later in the semester.

☼ **Put students to work.** What? Give them an assignment before I tell them all about my background, my expectations, and all of the other tedious details that they need to know? The answer is YES! Most definitely. A big mistake new teachers often make on the first day is to reveal too much information about themselves and the course without giving students a chance to participate. This first assignment should be low risk, one in which all students can be successful. Give them a journal assignment: "Please take about seven minutes to tell me about yourself." Students can't say that they don't know anything about the topic, and you will be sending the message that you are interested in them. Tell your students that it is important that you get acquainted so you can understand each other's background and expectations for the school year. After seven minutes, thank the students, and collect their papers. Your homework on the first night is to read these papers!

☼ **Avoid the "New Teacher Strut."** It's not a new line dance, but you can spot a new teacher every time when they do this little dance. It looks like this: the teacher stands in front of classroom, usually behind the overhead projector or a podium. The teacher's only foot movement during the entire period is three steps to the left or right from the starting position and back to center stage. Never does the teacher stray from this formation…UNLESS there is a fire drill. It may sound like an exaggeration, but this dance goes on all year for some teachers. Be aware that middle-school students are active and busy, and you need to know what they are doing at all times. Translated, YOU NEED TO MOVE AROUND THE CLASSROOM! Remember that it's hard to hit a moving target.

☼ **Teach procedures.** See Chapter 1 for information on the steps for teaching students your classroom procedures. Begin with the most important procedures, and build on those throughout the first week of school. Teaching students your procedures will communicate your expectation that the classroom will be an organized, efficient place.

☼ **RELAX!** Enjoy your first day.

Great Ideas for the First Days
of School from Experienced Teachers

Set the Right Tone

"During the first week of school, I try to set the tone for the rest of the year. I want the students to become comfortable with me and with each other, so team building is really essential. At the same time, I also want them to learn the rules of the classroom. It's quite a tricky task: I must set them on fire with enthusiasm, let them know that I am kind and that the classroom is a safe place, and at the same time, put the fear of Yeomanson into them so that 'discipline' will not be a problem later on! The message is mixed: **'I am fun! I am nice! Don't cross the line!!'**

For team-building, I do a variety of ice-breaking activities, such as **'Find Someone Who'** (see p. 57), team interviews, or name games. Generally, students do not like the spotlight to be on them in the beginning, so I put them into groups of four and give them a task. This introduces cooperative learning without being too threatening. I have found some good activities along these lines in a book called *Cooperative Group Problem Solving: Adventures in Applied Creativity* by Douglass Campbell (Frank Schaffer Publications, 1994; ISBN 0-86734-557-8).

I go over the classroom rules many times during the first week of school, and I make sure that I demonstrate the right and wrong ways of behaving. This has a double effect: I exaggerate to make my students laugh and put them at ease, plus they can see my expectations quite clearly. **It is not enough simply to print rules on a sign and leave it at that.** I also give 'fun' quizzes about the rules and award silly prizes. For example, I divide the class into two teams, and then have students line up to answer questions about classroom rules and procedures. The first person in line for each team races from the back of the classroom to the white board at the front of the room. The person who writes the answer on the board first earns a point for his/her team. Sample questions:

◆ Where do you place your homework when you enter the classroom?

◆ What happens if a student talks during a test?

◆ How many days will you have to make up assignments after an absence?

◆ What is the best way to get Mrs. Yeomanson's attention?

These quizzes reinforce the rules, but also serve as an introduction to the fact that students will have to become active learners."

—Victoria Yeomanson, English teacher

Procedures Precede Product

The most important step is to teach students your classroom procedures before making any attempt at teaching your content! Teach students how to behave and what is expected of them. Start with how you expect them to enter the classroom. You can ask students to volunteer to demonstrate or you can model the behavior yourself. Then have students practice the behavior and praise them when they have learned it. Demonstrate how to let you know—without verbal interruption—when they need a pencil, tissue, help, etc. Show students how to pass their papers across to the middle vertical row (or end row if preferred). Instruct them on how to be ready to work when the tardy bell rings and to have homework out on their desks to be checked or collected. Teach them how to find out what work they missed when absent (I use an Agenda Mate on the back wall with the week's assignments and a separate basket for each class for papers). I also hand out Student Interest forms for them to complete and then have them, on a volunteer basis, introduce themselves and read as much or as little from the form, as they like aloud to the class. This helps me get to know them better as well.

—*Patricia Revzin, English teacher*

During the first week of school, I mostly do team-building activities that raise awareness, teach tolerance, and prepare students for cooperative activities that involve problem-solving techniques. In addition, each day I spend a certain amount of time going over class procedures and practicing them.

—*Robin West, middle school teacher*

Interests as Icebreakers

On the first day of school, I give students an interest inventory. In addition to some biographical data, there are some open-ended statements such as, '*School would be better if...*' Their responses give me some insight into the students' interests and home life. On the second day we talk about the various types of activities students do in their classes, what they like and dislike, and then I explain learning styles. They take a Learning Style Inventory to determine their learning modalities, and I assure them that we will do varied activities—something for everyone— in the class. By the third day, we do an icebreaker activity, such as 'personality bingo,' or a hands-on project, such as balloon globes or crinkle maps. These activities give me some student work to display that first week of school.

—*Nancy Schneider, social studies teacher*

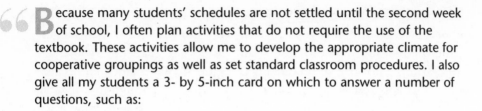

Because many students' schedules are not settled until the second week of school, I often plan activities that do not require the use of the textbook. These activities allow me to develop the appropriate climate for cooperative groupings as well as set standard classroom procedures. I also give all my students a 3- by 5-inch card on which to answer a number of questions, such as:

◆ What is your name?

◆ How many people are in your family?

◆ What is your shoe size?

◆ Do you like your toilet paper over or under?

◆ When is your birthday (month/day/year)?

◆ Do you have hair on the middle phalange of your ring finger?

These questions really pique students' interests, and they start thinking of the mathematics within these questions. While the questions are rich in mathematics, the main reason I have students fill out the cards is to learn when their birthdays are. I like to give little treats to students during the week of their birthday or "half-birthday," for those whose birthdays fall in the summer. Since I have students fill out the card during the first week, most do not remember filling it out and are surprised to find I know when their birthdays are.

—Eric Johnson, math teacher

Getting to Know Your Students

Wouldn't it be nice if we could know all about our students long before they arrive in our classroom on the first day? Imagine how helpful it would be to know their academic strengths and weak areas. We could individualize instruction so that we reach every student. We could choose materials that would best fit their needs and address their learning styles and interests.

In a perfect world, we would have months to plan our instruction. We would have weeks to develop the perfect lesson. In reality, we do long-range plans in advance of the first week of school, but we cannot really fine tune them until we meet the kids and gain an understanding of what knowledge, experience, and attitudes they bring with them to the classroom.

Like many experienced teachers, I find myself recreating units that I have taught in years past. Each year, it seems that the units are far from perfect because I need to address the students that I am currently teaching. After teaching American Literature for six years, I realized that I had three four-drawer filing cabinets full of supplementary materials for that course. I just couldn't teach it the same way every year. My students were different and so was I (thank goodness).

In some ways, we are all beginners each year we teach. That is why it is so important to get to know your students very quickly. Learn their names within the first few days of school—and go beyond that superficial information. Knowing your students is a great management tool because students usually respond well to a teacher who cares enough to know who they are. There are many ways for you to get acquainted with your students and for them to get to know each other. During the first days of school, it is wise to make these activities brief and in writing if possible; otherwise, you may find the attention-seeking students performing for the whole class— often in ways that are inappropriate. You can take their written autobiographies and interest surveys home to read at your leisure. Then, during the second and third weeks of school, you can introduce brief partner exchanges and small group activities that will help students learn your behavioral expectations as they learn about each other.

First, think about how you can learn about your students from what they will write. You can create your own Student Interest Survey, or use one of the ready-made, reproducible surveys provided in this chapter (pages 45–54). Gear your questions toward learning information about their interests, backgrounds, and attitudes about the subject that you teach. Remember that most of the other teachers will also be giving students an information sheet to fill out, so make your survey unique and fun. Explain to your students that you really want them to give you good information so that you can get to know them. Encourage them to take their time and be creative in their responses.

◀ *A student information survey can provide valuable information about your class.*

Student Interest Survey

Please print as neatly as possible!

Name: __Jessica__   Birthday: __March 4__

Adults who live with me:

Name __Joan (mom)__

Name __Brian (dad)__

Brothers and sisters:

Name __Carla__   Age __7__

Name _____   Age ____

Name _____   Age ____

Name _____   Age ____

(If you have more than four, please list others on the back of this sheet.)

Special friends: __Maria, Liz, Brittany, Min__

What I like to do most at home: __watch TV__

My favorite hobbies: __softball, photography__

Student Interest Survey

Please print as neatly as possible!

Name: _____ Birthday: _____

Adults who live with me:

Name _____

Name _____

Brothers and sisters:

Name _____ Age _____

Name _____ Age _____

Name _____ Age _____

Name _____ Age _____

(If you have more than four, please list others on the back of this sheet.)

Special friends: _____

_____

What I like to do most at home: _____

_____

My favorite hobbies: _____

_____

Student Interest Survey (Page 2)

My favorite book(s) and magazine(s): _____

_____

If I had one wish, it would be... _____

_____

School would be better if... _____

_____

If I had a million dollars, I would... _____

_____

One thing that I am really good at is... _____

_____

I do my best thinking when... _____

_____

This is what one of my teachers did last year that I liked the most: _____

_____

This is what one of my teachers did last year that I liked the least: _____

_____

The New Teacher's Complete Sourcebook: Middle School Scholastic Professional Books

Student Interest Survey (Page 3)

After I graduate, I want to... _____

_____

Something else that I want you to know about me is... _____

_____

_____

_____

My All-Time Favorites:

☼ candy: _____

☼ movie: _____

☼ song: _____

☼ musical group: _____

☼ type of pizza:_____

☼ color: _____

☼ car: _____

☼ professional athletic team:_____

☼ style of clothing: _____

☼ vacation place: _____

☼ board game: _____

☼ radio station:_____

☼ TV show:_____

☼ outdoor activity:_____

Language Arts

Name: _____ Period: _____

Birthday: _____

Parent/Guardian Name: _____

Telephone: _____

What is your favorite book? _____

_____

What do you like to read in your spare time? _____

_____

If you could have only one magazine subscription, what would you choose?

_____

What type of movies do you enjoy? _____

_____

What are some lyrics of your favorite song? _____

_____

_____

_____

The New Teacher's Complete Sourcebook: Middle School   Scholastic Professional Books

Language Arts (Page 2)

What TV commercial sticks in your mind? Why? _____

_____

_____

How often do you write in a journal or diary?

_____ Daily   _____ Occasionally   _____ Never

Write one word that describes you for each letter of your first name. For example, if your name is Erica…

Energetic, **R**unner, **I**nteresting, **C**aring, **A**thlete

_____

_____

For each of the following words, give a slang term that you might use when speaking with your friends or people your age. For example, for friend, you might put "buddy."

✧ Friend_____

✧ Good _____

✧ Bad _____

What do I need to know about you to help you be successful in this class?

_____

_____

_____

Mathematics

Name: _____ Period: _____

Birthday: _____

Parent/Guardian Name: _____

Telephone: _____

What is your lucky number? Explain how you know that it is lucky for you.

_____

How old were you on your millennium birthday (January 1, 2000 to December 31, 2000)**?**

_____

If you could make up the name of the largest known number, what would you call it?

_____

If you had one hundred extra dollars, how would you spend it? _____

_____

What is the fastest way to get from your house to school?
(For example: Go west on Pebble Street until you get to Eastern Avenue. Then turn right...)

_____

_____

_____

Do you have a collection? If so, what do you collect? _____

What do I need to know about you to help you be successful in this class? _____

_____

_____

The New Teacher's Complete Sourcebook: Middle School Scholastic Professional Books

Science

Name: _____ **Period:** _____

Birthday: _____

Parent/Guardian Name: _____

Telephone: _____

Please list your favorites:

☼ sport _____

☼ athletic team _____

☼ clothes _____

☼ candy _____

☼ after-school snack _____

☼ game (board game or video game)_____

☼ television show _____

What is one invention that you could not live without?

_____

_____

How do you think science is related to your everyday life?

_____

_____

_____

Science (Page 2)

When you are trying to solve a problem or figure something out, which strategies do you like to use? (Check all that apply.)

_____ Read the directions

_____ Ask a parent or older sibling for help

_____ Call a friend

_____ Ask a teacher

_____ Look on the Internet

_____ Look in a textbook

_____ Give up and do something else

_____ Try again later

If you could be an animal, what would you be and why?

_____

_____

_____

What do I need to know about you to help you be successful in this class?

_____

_____

_____

_____

The New Teacher's Complete Sourcebook: Middle School   Scholastic Professional Books

Social Studies

Name: _____ Period: _____

Birthday: _____

Parent/Guardian Name: _____

Telephone: _____

Imagine that someday you are famous because you are listed in the *Guinness Book of World Records.* For what great feat might you hold a world record?

_____

If you could speak with a famous person (either from today or from history) who would you choose? What question would you ask this person?

_____

_____

_____

To what places have you traveled? _____

_____

If you could take a first-class vacation to anywhere in the world, where would you go? Why?

_____

_____

_____

Social Studies (Page 2)

When you recall how to get from your house to another place, do you remember street names or landmarks?

_____

Some people think that "two is company and three is a crowd." If that is true, then what is

one? _____ four? _____

If you could live during any decade of the 1900's, which decade would you choose, and why?

_____

_____

Write the word that comes first to your mind when you hear the following terms:

✩ adventure _____

✩ war _____

✩ invention _____

✩ America _____

✩ freedom _____

✩ success _____

What do I need to know about you to help you be successful in this class?

_____

_____

_____

The New Teacher's Complete Sourcebook: Middle School   Scholastic Professional Books

Why You Need Team-Building Activities

When you observe a group of middle-school students interacting, either in the school cafeteria or in the corridors, you may wonder how they manage to get along with each other. The truth is that often they don't get along—even with their friends. Imagine what happens when thirty or more students are thrown together in a classroom. It is unrealistic to expect a group of 11- to 15-year-old strangers to cooperate automatically and treat each other with respect and courtesy. Yet with careful planning, effective teachers establish a sense of community in their classrooms by using team-building activities.

Team-building activities address the following questions:

- What do we have in common?

- How is each member unique and valued by the other members of the class?

- How can we accomplish more by working together?

As students interact with each other in ways that foster respect and acceptance, they can begin to develop trust—a necessary component of cooperative learning. Team-building activities give students a chance to talk with each other about things that really matter to them: their interests, hobbies, past experiences, and other important aspects of their lives. Select team-building activities that are fun and relevant to your course curriculum, if possible. Use your imagination, but remember that the goal is to help students discover what they have in common and to value each other's unique personalities.

Sample Ice-Breakers and Team-Building Activities

- **Partner Interviews and Introductions:** Students interview partners using a form (similar to the one on page 58). Partners may then introduce one another to the class.

- **Alike/Different Activity:** Students work together in a small group to discover three things that all members have in common and one thing that is unique to each. Allow students to ask the questions and discover the common threads on their own. Sample question: "Is there a particular television show that we all like to watch?" Each team reports their findings to the class.

☼ **People Bingo:** Create a "People Bingo" game for your students using indicators such as "has brown eyes," "plays basketball," "rides bus to school," and "likes to skateboard." Allow teammates to initial the boxes that apply to them. The first team to score three boxes in a row, column, or diagonal wins. Next time, allow students to create their own "People Bingo."

☼ **True or False?** Each student writes three statements about himself/herself, two of which are false and one that is true. Students ask teammates to guess which statement is true.

☼ **Design a Team Motto, Logo, Crest, or T-shirt:** To create an esprit de corps, have students work together in small groups to create a team symbol to convey their identity to the larger group. This activity can be done in many ways and can incorporate your course curriculum if you weave it into a lesson. For example, in an English class, students may create a motto using literary devices, such as alliteration or allusion, learned in class. Display team symbols or mottos on the walls.

Students' t-shirts show their unique interests, talents, and personalities.

Name: _____

Find Someone Who...

Please move around the classroom and talk to one another to find someone who fits each description. Have that person sign on the line. **You may only use a person's name twice on your sheet. You may not sign your own sheet.** When you are finished, please bring your sheet to me. If you are the winner, we will verify that each person who signed your sheet can answer the corresponding question or perform the task. Please print your name legibly!

1. saw his or her grandmother over the summer _____

2. knows the name of the school's principal _____

3. can stand on his/her head _____

4. knows what a noun is _____

5. is wearing something white _____

6. knows how many days are in the school year _____

7. knows the value of *pi* _____

8. writes poetry _____

9. can name five animals that begin with the letter A _____

10. was born in a state east of the Mississippi _____

11. has the same birthday month as you _____

12. has more than four siblings _____

13. ate waffles for breakfast this morning _____

14. can sing four lines from an N' Sync song without laughing _____

15. knows the capital of Maine _____

Partner Interview

Complete this chart for yourself, then interview two partners. How are you all alike?
Be ready to introduce one of your partners to the class.

	MY NAME:	PARTNER'S NAME:	PARTNER'S NAME:
1 Your middle name			
2 Favorite fast food			
3 Favorite candy bar			
4 Favorite book			
5 Favorite team			
6 Favorite color			
7 Most treasured possession			
8 Favorite class in school			
9 Favorite CD			
10 Place you were born			

The New Teacher's Complete Sourcebook: Middle School   Scholastic Professional Books

"Getting to Know You" Team-Building Activity

Objective:

To encourage participants to get acquainted and communicate with each other by sharing personal information with peers in a non-threatening environment.

Materials/Set Up:

☼ Class Norms Poster (made in advance; see example on next page.)

☼ Questions for discussion (about eight or nine questions, beginning with low-risk, and moving to more thought-provoking or personal questions. See examples on page 61.)

☼ Chairs (not desks) set up in two lines facing each other. Use an equal number of chairs. If you have an odd number of participants, then you must sit down and participate in the activity as well as facilitate. No one should be left out of this activity.

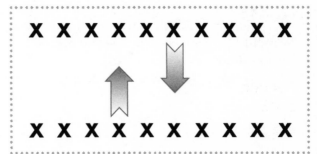

Time:

About 30 minutes

Procedure:

1. Arrange students so they are seated across from someone they do not know. Each student should be face-to-face with a partner. The entire group should be seated side by side facing another line of students who are sitting side by side. Ask students to introduce themselves to the person across from them and to shake hands. For best results, you must model this with a student before having the students do this step.

2. Explain to the group that in order for group activities to be successful, there need to be some "norms" or ground rules in place. Refer to a list of norms that you have printed on the board or on a poster. Explain the norms and clarify them by asking students questions such as, "What does respectful listening look like?" or "What would I expect to see if I were watching two people and they were listening respectfully to each other?" Possible answers may include: *nodding, eye contact, leaning toward the person,* or *smiling.* Then ask, "What does respectful

(Continued on next page)

"Getting to Know You" Team-Building Activity
(Continued)

listening sound like?" or "What would I expect to hear if I were listening to two people respectfully communicating with each other?" Answers may include the following: *only one person speaking at a time*, or *follow-up questions being asked*. Try to get students to generate concrete examples so they have a clear understanding of your expectations. Make sure that the norms are simple and age appropriate. For this activity, an example of class norms for a middle-school setting may be the following:

Obtain agreement from all students that they are able and willing to abide by the norms.

Class Norms

1. Respect
2. Confidentiality
3. Right to Pass
4. Participate
5. Have fun!

3. Instruct participants that you will ask a question, and they are to discuss the answer to that question with their partners. They must take turns speaking and follow the class norms. Explain that you will be giving a signal when it is time to stop talking after each discussion. The signal will be, "PLEASE, thank your partner, and MOVE TO THE RIGHT."

4. Ask the first question and allow sufficient time for discussion of the question. Noise level in the room will decrease as participants are finished with each question. Usually I allow about two minutes, but it depends on the question. Use the signal: "PLEASE, thank your partner and MOVE TO THE RIGHT."

5. Participants will move one seat to their right, and then you will ask the next question. Encourage participants to introduce themselves and shake hands with their new partner. Repeat the process until all questions are discussed.

(Continued on next page)

"Getting to Know You" Team-Building Activity
(Continued)

6. Debrief after the activity, while participants are still seated. During this discussion, ask participants the following questions, and try to get more than one person to respond:

◆ How do you feel about this activity? What made you feel that way?

◆ What did you notice about the way your classmates behaved?

◆ Which question did you like, and why did you like it?

◆ What did you gain from participating in this activity?

Explain that the interactions that you observed were very respectful and that you hope to see students continue to treat each other this way when they work cooperatively during academic tasks in the classroom. Thank students for their participation.

NOTE: As you plan the questions that you will ask, begin with very low-risk ones. Your questions should become progressively more "risky" for students to answer.

Sample Questions

You may need to revise these questions to make them age appropriate and of interest to the participants in your class.

✪ What is your favorite food? Why?

✪ What is your favorite movie? Why?

✪ What is your favorite sports team? Why?

✪ What is the best book you have ever read? Why?

✪ Tell about a place you would like to visit.

✪ Finish this statement: "I have fun when…"

✪ Tell your partner about your best friend.

✪ Tell your partner about your family.

✪ Who is the person you most admire? Why?

✪ If you had one wish, what would it be?

Opposites Attract

This simple activity is a good ice-breaker to use at the beginning of the school year or when returning from a track break, if you teach on a year-round schedule. It is a way of allowing students to connect with each other and to establish common ground.

Before giving the directions for this activity, select some upbeat music to play while students are moving around to find a partner and while they talk to each other in response to the prompts you will provide. Good traveling music might be something like "In the Mood," "Great Balls of Fire," or "Happy Together."

Directions:

Please stand up and push in your chair. In just a minute, when I say "Go," everyone will take at least ten steps from where they are now standing. When you hear the music stop, please find someone standing near you to be your partner. Ready, set, GO. (Play music for 30 seconds.)

Now, with your partner, please find something about each other that is obviously different. For example, you may have short hair and your partner has long hair. Talk to your partner now to find a way in which you are different. (Play music for 20 seconds.) Stop the music, then ask for a few volunteers to share how they are different.

Now with your partner, find another, less obvious way that you are different. For example, you may like to play video games in your spare time and your partner may like to skate (play music for 30 seconds). Stop the music, and ask for a few volunteers to share how they are different.

Now that you know how you are different from each other, try to find at least three things that you have in common (play music for about one minute). Stop the music, and again ask for a few volunteers to share what they have in common.

During the semester (trimester, or school year) we will be working together on assignments and projects. In order to cooperate, we need to appreciate each other's unique personalities and learning styles. After all, "How boring the world would be, if everyone were just like me."

Thank students for participating in this activity. Then ask students to thank their partners and return to their seats. Play music while students travel to their seats.

Establishing Classroom Rules

Rules are different from procedures. You need both in order to have a smooth-running, orderly classroom. Rules set up your expectations for student behavior, whereas procedures indicate how things are to be done in the classroom. Refer to Chapter 1 for an in-depth discussion of how to teach classroom procedures to your students.

You might think that by the time a student reaches the sixth grade, he or she should know what the school and classroom rules are. However, many students view each teacher's classroom as a separate entity; after all, each teacher has a unique personality with a temperament that differs from other teachers in the same school building. The way that you establish your classroom rules and how you enforce those rules will contribute to or detract from the business of learning.

You don't need to ask your students if they behave the same in every class. Teachers who teach on a team quickly learn that some students are as good as gold in one class and off the wall in another. There are many variables that impact student behavior, but there are several factors over which teachers have control. What makes a student want to participate and be cooperative in a classroom? It boils down to a very simple fact: The teacher sets the tone for the classroom.

Why are rules necessary?

Rules tell students what the limits are in your classroom. Your rules may be different from the rules of other teachers that the students have. Therefore, your rules need to be clearly stated, explained, and posted for students' reference. Include your rules in your course expectations so parents are aware of the behavior expectations in your classroom. Teachers who set limits are not mean; rather, they are providing structure and a sense of security for students. School must be a safe and orderly place where students can come to learn without being afraid.

What should my rules be?

You may want to get examples of other teachers' rules, but refrain from copying and using them if they do not fit your style. Think about what is important to you in terms of classroom management and what you can and cannot tolerate. For instance, some teachers do not mind if students get up to sharpen their pencils without permission. Consider some examples of specific rules from veteran teachers.

Sample Classroom Rules

Here are sample rules from experienced teachers:

1. Treat all members of our learning community with respect.

2. Please use the restroom before or after class. Passes will be given for emergencies only.

3. We begin on time. Students who are not in their seats when the bell rings will be marked tardy. Students who are tardy will not be allowed to turn in homework that has already been collected, receive handouts that have already been distributed, and/or take quizzes or tests that are already in progress.

4. Please consume all food and beverages OUTSIDE the classroom.

5. Dismissal from class will occur in a civilized manner. Please remain in your seats until you hear me say, "Have a great day!"

1. Be on time.
2. Be prepared.
3. Do class work and homework.
4. Be kind to your classmates and teacher.

The rules will be enforced in this classroom. The one rule to follow is **DO NOT EXHIBIT ANY BEHAVIOR THAT IN ANY WAY INTERFERES WITH INSTRUCTION OR THE LEARNING PROCESS.**

Expectations:

1. Demonstrate courtesy and respect to ALL members of the class, including the instructor.

2. Be cautious in the laboratory and abide by all safety rules.

3. Do not bring nuisance items to class or they may be confiscated.

4. Until you can demonstrate satisfactory completion of your biology work, do not work on material from another class or activity. YOU MUST WORK EACH DAY UNTIL THE BELL RINGS—DO NOT PUT AWAY LEARNING MATERIALS EARLY!

5. Always put forth your full effort in class.

—Mary Pike, science teacher

(Excerpt from course expectation sheet)

Classroom Management: Mutual Courtesy/Mutual Respect

I have the right to teach, and students have the right to learn; therefore, anything done to disrupt this process will be considered a discipline problem and will be handled accordingly. Participation points may also be lost.

1. Respect others and their property.

2. Be in assigned seat before the tardy bell rings, and remain there unless otherwise instructed.

3. Remain on task.

4. Bring appropriate materials to class every day.

5. When you are absent, you are responsible for your own make-up work.

6. When a student misbehaves, the following sequence of consequences will be employed:

   1. Warning   2. After-school detention   3. Phone call home   4. Referral to dean

Any student severely disrupting the class will be immediately sent to the dean.

7. A student who behaves appropriately will earn

   1. Verbal praise   2. Positive calls home   3. Award and/or certificate

—Eric Johnson, math teacher

Guidelines for Rule-Making

- ☼ When possible, state your rules in positive terms, rather than beginning every rule with "Don't…"

- ☼ Try to limit your rules to no more than five.

- ☼ Explain the rules clearly to your students.

- ☼ Review the rules several times during the first week of school and periodically throughout the semester.

- ☼ Identify the consequences for breaking classroom rules.

- ☼ Post your rules on a wall in your classroom.

- ☼ Include classroom rules in your course expectations.

Introducing Your Classroom Rules

You may want to find a creative way to introduce your classroom rules to your students. Remember that they have six teachers who are all probably standing in front of them on the first day of school reading the rules. Effective teachers have a way of making the rules meaningful for their particular classroom. For example, two children's picture books containing themes related to rules that can be used to grab your students' attention are *The Teacher from the Black Lagoon* by Mike Thaler, or *Miss Nelson Is Missing* by Harry Allard.

◀ *A clear set of classroom rules lets everyone know what to expect.*

Another interesting way to get the attention of your students is to teach them about Howard Gardner's research on multiple intelligences (*Intelligence Reframed: Multiple Intelligences for the 21st Century*, Basic Books, 2000), and after giving them a profile on their strengths, allow them to illustrate your classroom rules using each of the multiple intelligences. For example, if the rule is "Respect each other," then consider how that rule would be communicated using each of the following multiple intelligences:

- **Verbal-Linguistic** (slogan, speech, dialogue, editorial, debate)

- **Logical-Mathematical** (solving problems, giving reasons for rules, classifying rules)

- **Visual-Spatial** (poster, mind map, drawing, sculpture, logo, flyer)

- **Musical-Rhythmic** (team cheer, rap, song, jingle)

- **Bodily-Kinesthetic** (role-play, Pictionary™, charades)

- **Interpersonal** (game, skit, partner work, talk show)

- **Intrapersonal** (reflection, journal, goal setting, self-assessment)

Discipline—Wonka Style

On the third day of school, I introduce my discipline policy to my students. I approach my explanation the same way I approach discipline all year long; I am unemotional, non-threatening, and I do not spend too much time on it. To emphasize my approach, I show a short clip from the movie *Willy Wonka and the Chocolate Factory*. It is the part where Willy Wonka demonstrates his amazing machine that produces a three-course meal within a piece of gum. A child grabs the gum out of his hand (misbehavior). Wonka calmly advises her, 'Ah, I wouldn't do that.' She persists and starts chewing the gum (continued misbehavior). Without any emotion, Wonka quietly warns, 'No, stop, don't.' The girl continues chewing and eventually turns into a giant blueberry.

'Why didn't Wonka scream, yell, and become angry when the child broke a rule?' I ask. The response from the class is, 'He knew what was going to happen.' Then I say, 'Please, do not wait for me to scream and yell to let you know there will be a consequence for breaking the rules because I will not do that, but there will still be a consequence.' I then spend a few minutes explaining my discipline program. The trick is having a solid discipline program in place and remaining calm when you must enforce the rules and consequences.

—*Mark Heywood, English teacher*

Involving Students in Making the Rules

If you want your students to abide by the rules, then allow them to be involved in establishing what the rules are in the classroom. Set the parameters for this activity by discussing why rules are necessary in society. You may ask them, "What would happen if there were no laws?" Make sure that students understand that the classroom rules cannot contradict school rules such as the dress code and tardy policy. If, for example, your school has a "gum-free" environment policy, then of course, your students are expected to be "gum-free" in your classroom.

One way to establish a climate of community is to guide students through the process of forming the rules. You can accomplish this task through a cooperative group activity where students brainstorm the type of environment where optimal learning can take place. The rule-making activity can be a springboard into the content of your class if you are teaching social studies, literature, science, or mathematics. All of these disciplines require some type of law and order, whether it is the natural laws of physics, or the order of operations in math. In physical education, there are numerous examples of rules in sports, and in history there are examples of societies that struggled with the process of establishing common rules by which all members must abide. Consider using an excerpt from literature to introduce your classroom rules:

- ☼ *The Sneetches and Other Stories*, by Dr. Seuss

- ☼ *The Giver*, by Lois Lowry

- ☼ *Matilda*, by Roald Dahl

- ☼ *Harry Potter and the Sorcerer's Stone*, by J.K. Rowling

◄ *Engaging students in the rule-making process can establish a positive tone in the classroom.*

Student-Generated Classroom Rules

Objective:

To let students take ownership of the rules, thereby giving them more desire to follow them.

Procedure:

Choose a recorder to write student responses on the board. Ask students to give examples of rules that they think should be followed in a classroom. I like to guide students to rules that are stated in positive terms.

- ☼ Be positive.

- ☼ Be courteous.

- ☼ Be creative.

- ☼ Be on time.

- ☼ Be prepared.

After the class votes on the rules, they can work together in small groups to create posters that represent the class rules.

—Carrie Boehlecke, English teacher

If you prefer to set the rules ahead of time, then you may want to involve your students by having a cooperative activity where small groups internalize the rules by drawing diagrams or sketches of their interpretation of the rules. You may allow the students to vote for the best student-made rule posters. Winners might receive a candy bar or a special pencil set as a prize. Label and post their drawings so that when you need to review the rules, you can refer to their interpretations. Obviously, there will be more than one way to interpret the rules, so include all drawings that are appropriate. These drawings will also be a colorful and inexpensive way to decorate your room prior to Open House.

Tip

Know what you want your class rules to be before you begin this activity!

CHAPTER 4

Effective
Planning
and Lesson Design:

It *Does* Make
a Difference!

Planning effective instruction is time-consuming for beginning (and high-performing veteran) teachers. When I was a new teacher, I thought if only I could have access to the magic filing cabinet of the best English teacher in my school, then planning would be so fast and easy. What I soon realized is that there is so much variation among students that my planning had to be informed, flexible, and supportive of the needs and interests of my learners. For me, it is impossible to use generic lesson plans created by another teacher without adjusting and adapting them. It just doesn't work. However, it is not necessary to reinvent the wheel. There are certainly great teaching ideas from educators within your building and district; you just have to reach out and ask for their contributions.

Many teachers find, as I did, that when you teach the same course a second or third year in a row, you are constantly tinkering with your unit plans and fine-tuning your instructional strategies as you go. Although effective planning and lesson design never ends, it does get easier with time and experience. In this chapter, you will find tips on long-range planning, essential components for effective lesson plans, and suggestions for incorporating a variety of strategies into your instructional design. As you gain confidence and experience, it won't be long before a new teacher will think that you have a magic filing cabinet.

Where Do I Start?

Now that you have received your teaching assignment and the textbooks for the course that you will be teaching, you may feel a little overwhelmed. Where do you start? An important item that will help you stay on track during the school year is the **benchmarks** for your course. Hopefully your state department of education or your school district has created a list of skills that students are supposed to have mastered by certain points in their school career. With your course benchmarks or your state standards in hand, you can sit down and plan the **major units** that you will cover during the year. If you have not received the following items from your school administrator, ask for them immediately:

- ☼ Course Curriculum Guide

- ☼ State Standards for the course

- ☼ Benchmarks

- ☼ Textbooks and Teacher's Manuals

- ☼ Supplementary materials

You can avoid the trap of day-to-day planning by sketching out the entire year at once. Begin by obtaining a calendar. I find it helpful to use a computer-generated one for the months of September through June with daily squares large enough to fit titles of units and important school events. Be sure to mark out all of the holidays and other school events, as these are potential interruptions to your unit and daily lesson plans.

Some events to note include:

1. Beginning and end of quarters or trimesters

2. Semester exam dates

3. School holidays and religious holidays

4. Standardized testing dates

5. School events (team days, field trips, homecoming, assemblies, etc.)

6. Staff development days

7. Picture days, health testing, etc.

It is amazing how many instructional days are impacted by the business of running a school. When you look at the remaining days, you realize how precious the time is!

Sketching Out the Year

Once I have an overview of my academic year, I begin sketching my unit plan onto the calendar. Using the course syllabus, I plot out my units in general terms (one week for one unit, three weeks for another, etc.). I always use PENCIL when doing this preliminary planning. If I run out of time, I go back and shave off weeks/days in units until I feel I have reasonably mapped out my year for the course syllabus. Once I finish this, I can become more specific and tie my objectives into my textbook and other materials. When I write the learning objective in my plan book, I also write the school district's corresponding curriculum objective number in a corner of the book. This helps me know what I have covered!

Sometimes new teachers feel they have to cover the entire textbook in their course. Instead, it makes more sense to use the textbook as a resource for covering your syllabus. It may sound obvious, but you would be surprised how many experienced teachers are plowing through their textbooks, page by page, and falling short of the required course objectives at the end of the school year. If you have a general plan at the beginning, and follow the course curriculum guide established by your school district, you will have a more organized, successful year and not feel so 'rushed' as May draws to a close.

—*Nancy Schneider, social studies teacher*

You Are Not Alone! Seek Help from Experienced Teachers

If this is your first year of teaching a particular course, it is wise to *talk to other teachers in your school who have taught the class before*. They will be able to guide you in deciding how much time to spend on certain concepts and how you can structure the course to ensure that you meet the benchmarks and address your state standards. Ask these veteran teachers which skills the students generally need to review and practice at the beginning of the year. For example, do not assume that since your students had seventh grade English the year before that they are completely familiar and at ease with the writing process and know how to correctly punctuate a sentence when you get them in eighth grade. Somehow, over the summer, students forget many of the basics! Experienced teachers will usually have good ideas on how to review key concepts quickly and bring students up to speed. You don't have to teach the course exactly like the teacher next door, but pay attention to his advice. He has been there and done that!

If your middle school utilizes **teaming**, then you will need to meet with the other teachers on your team to discuss any interdisciplinary units that you will plan together. Teams usually consist of teachers from each of the disciplines—math, science, reading, English, and social studies—who teach the same group of students. Depending on the philosophy of your principal, you may be required to do a certain number of interdisciplinary units each year. For example, in one middle school, the 8th grade World History teacher and the English teacher coordinate their plans so that students simultaneously read literature relating to the countries that are being studied in the World History class. At the end of each semester, students create projects and presentations as culminating activities for the units that they have studied in these two classes.

Why Plan Units?

Here are a few advantages to planning your own instructional units at the beginning of the school year:

- ☼ Unit planning provides an overview of the entire year and shows how you will fit major topics and specific concepts together. You will see the "big picture."

- ☼ You will be able to work on lesson plans *in advance*. Once you have one unit thoroughly planned for several weeks, you can begin to work on future units.

- ☼ Having specific unit plans keeps you organized as you gather materials and ideas to enhance future units.

- ☼ You will avoid the exhaustion of trying to come up with the next thing to teach from day to day or week to week.

- ☼ As you plan ahead, you will be able to incorporate a variety of teaching materials and strategies instead of resorting to repetitious worksheets.

- ☼ You will be more confident knowing that you stand a better chance of covering all the important content and goals because you have planned the time carefully.

See a sample of one science teacher's overview of units on page 75. Since she knows what's happening when, she can gather materials and create lessons and activities well in advance. I highly recommend taking time early in the year to map out the units you'd like to teach. Check out the Guidelines for Planning Units on page 76.

◀ *Students become deeply involved in exploring units of study.*

Sample Year-at-a-Glance Unit Plans

Physical Science, Grade 8
Thumbnail Sketch of Units

FIRST SEMESTER

Introduction to Science (three weeks)

History of Science
Scientific Method
Metric System
Measurement
Laboratory Skills
Process Skills

Matter (three weeks)

General Properties
States of Matter
Physical and Chemical Properties

Atoms (three weeks)

Elements and Compounds
Chemical Reactions
Building Atom Models

Energy (four weeks)

Forms and Sources
Kinetic Energy
Potential Energy
Conservation
Nuclear Energy
Research and Presentations: Searching
    for Solutions to the Energy Crisis

Forces and Motion (four weeks)

Objects and Speed
Newton's Laws
Gravitation
Pressure, Density, and Buoyancy
Egg Drop Contest

SECOND SEMESTER

Machines and Work (four weeks)

Work
Simple Machines
Compound Machines
Mechanical Advantage
Mouse Trap Car Races

Electricity (four weeks)

Electric Charge
Circuits
Magnetic Properties/Electromagnetism
Field Trip to Lied Discovery Museum
Building Hands-On Science Discovery Exhibits
    for Third-Grade Science Museum

Waves (two weeks)

Properties
Motion
Electromagnetic Spectrum

Sound (two weeks)

Properties & Characteristics

Light (two weeks)

Nature of Light
Visible Spectrum
Optics
Laser Light Show (student-generated show
    performed at school Learning Festival)

Careers in Science and Technology (three weeks)

Student Research
Student-Created PowerPoint Presentations
Guest Speakers
Field Trip to University Science Center

Guidelines for Planning Units

1. Become familiar with your school district's curriculum guide, benchmarks, and state standards for the course you are teaching.

2. List the major curriculum categories.

3. Summarize the curriculum by listing single concepts within these major categories.

4. Make a list of the concepts being taught in these categories in both the grade level above and the grade level below the one you are currently teaching. This gives you a good sense of continuum, helps you become more informed when answering parental questions, and saves you planning time if you teach a different grade level in the future.

5. Select the category you will teach first. Combine any concepts that are appropriate to teach together and arrange the concepts using any of the following criteria:

   ◆ Obvious chronological, sequential, ascending, or descending order

   ◆ Availability of materials

   ◆ Your teaching style

6. Use a three-ring binder to organize your course materials by units.

7. Locate teaching materials appropriate for each concept, such as relevant newspaper articles, trade books, Internet web sites, field trip information, and lists of guest speakers. Include all materials that you find that might relate to the concept (it's easier to discard or return materials than to relocate them later). Because your students' needs will vary from class to class, it is a good idea to keep a wide variety of materials on hand.

8. Sketch out your unit plan by listing the concepts, objectives, and expected student outcomes. (See the sample Mythology Unit included in this chapter.)

9. Review all materials gathered for each concept and list those you actually plan to use.

10. Break the unit into lessons containing learning activities that match curriculum objectives. Gather ideas for student projects, demonstrations, problem-solving activities, and other hands-on learning activities.

Take a look at a sample unit plan on pages 78–84.

Effective teachers ask themselves these two essential questions when planning a unit:

1 What do I want my students to know or be able to do at the end of the unit?

2 How will I know if they know it or are able to do it?

The answer to the first question comes from your school district's course curriculum guide. In most districts, a committee of experienced teachers and administrators has written the curriculum guides. The course you are teaching is carefully aligned with the courses students will have taken before and after it. It is wise to stay within the guidelines outlined in your course curriculum so students will be well-prepared for the next course in the sequence of classes they will take during middle and high school. Try to view the curriculum guide requirements as a *minimum* level of student competencies. Most important, be flexible, and remember to challenge all students to reach their potential. Never water down your curriculum in the name of remediation. To help all students really succeed, challenge them with meaningful learning experiences in which they must apply information and actively solve problems.

A student uses the Internet to explore ancient Greece.

Mythology

Prepared by Jeanne Mulligan
Middle-School Language Arts Teacher

Rationale:

Mythological stories can be traced across continents and back to the beginning of time. People from different cultures have created myths to celebrate the diverse, the heroic, the unbelievable, and the unknown. At first glance, students may wonder what ties their lives may have to Greek mythology, if any. However, upon further examination, they will realize that myths have provided us with explanations, have influenced our vocabulary, have entertained people for many generations, and continue to teach us many lessons.

Goals:

Students will gain knowledge and understanding of

- ☼ the legacy of ancient Greece,
- ☼ selected myths, gods, and goddesses and their impact on literature today,
- ☼ and the relationship between Greek mythology and modern society.

Curricular Objectives (partial list):

1. develop skills needed to respond to inferential and critical questions when reading
2. utilize works of literature as springboards to writing
3. develop vocabulary
4. develop oral and written skills
5. compare and contrast Greek mythology to other stories
6. practice writing for a variety of purposes and audiences
7. identify elements of Greek mythology in popular culture, including advertising, humorous writing, fiction, and product identification

Length of Unit:

Approximately four weeks

(Continued on next page)

Unit Launch (Lesson Plan for the First Day of the Unit)

1. Teacher will enter the classroom wearing a toga over his or her normal "mortal" school clothes and begin class, in character, as a chosen god/goddess. For example, she may start as follows:

> *Hello, and welcome to Mount Olympus. I am the goddess Athena, the daughter of Zeus, who is the supreme ruler. I sprang full-grown in armor from the forehead of Zeus; thus, I have no mother. I am fierce and brave in battle, and I am the goddess of the city, handicrafts, and agriculture. I invented the bridle, which permitted man to tame horses. I also invented the trumpet, the flute, the rake, the plow, the ship, and the chariot. I am the embodiment of wisdom, reason, and purity. I am my father's favorite child, and I am even allowed to use his weapons, including his thunderbolt. My favorite city is Athens, and my tree is the olive. The owl is my bird. Come with me and my brothers and sisters of Greek mythology, and we will guide you on a magical journey through our land and our stories.*

2. Next, (no longer in character as a god/goddess) the teacher leads a **K-W-L** activity to assess the students' prior knowledge. For the "K" or KNOW segment, the teacher will ask, *What do we know about mythology, and how do these stories relate to our lives?* Students will list all of the information that they currently know about mythology.

KNOW	**WONDER**	**LEARN**
What *do we know about* mythology, and *how do these stories relate to our lives?*	What *do we wonder or want to learn about* mythology or the Greek gods/goddesses?	What have we learned about mythology?
Cupid—he's the god of love and we see him on Valentine's Day Atlantis the movie has something to do with mythology		

(Continued on next page)

3. The teacher will explain to students: *Myths were the main form of education for Greeks long ago, and because of this, they represent more than the charming stories of an ancient culture. The stories were the basis for great classical works because they carried significance for humankind. The myths revealed the nature of relationships between parents and children and they explained, among many other things, why evil exists alongside or together with good.*

The teacher should ask, *What other forms of writing have we studied this year that are similar to myths?* Students should be able to give examples of fables that were studied.

4. The teacher can then show examples of products that we use today that contain mythological references: Ajax cleaner, cereal (after Ceres, the goddess of agriculture), FTD's florist symbol of Hermes/Mercury, and Nike athletic shoes. Teachers might invite students to speculate as to why these gods and goddesses are associated with these products.

5. Then, after creating a list of deities from Greek mythology, the teacher can ask if students have heard of any of these gods or goddesses. Students will generate questions for the "W" or WONDER part of the K-W-L. *What do you wonder about mythology and these characters?*

6. The teacher will model the process of filling out a Mythological Character Chart for Athena, asking for students' input. The chart will contain information relating to the following aspects of character:

- God's/goddess' domain or influence
- Superhuman qualities, strengths, or talents
- Parents or family relations
- Personality quirks or flaws
- Symbols that represent the god or goddess (for example the owl represents Athena's wisdom)

7. The students will then choose the name of a god or goddess from a cornucopia (purple for girls and green for boys). This will be the god that they represent for the duration of the thematic unit. They will research their god or goddess and fill in their own Character Chart during class. Throughout the days of this unit, students will be creating items for their mythology scrapbook. The items will be related to the god or goddess that they select on this first day of the unit.

8. The teacher will explain the rest of the mythology unit, so students will know what to expect over the next few weeks. Students will choose dates for giving their oral presentations, which will be in character of the god or goddess they represent and will describe what makes the god/goddess special (similar to the teacher's presentation at the beginning of this unit).

9. Finally, at the end of the class period, students will write in their journals about what they liked most during class or something new they have learned.

(Continued on next page)

Learning Activities for Mythology Unit

I. K-W-L: This activity is used at the beginning of the unit to assess how much students already know about mythology and to determine what they would be interested in learning. At the conclusion of the unit, students work in small groups to generate lists of **new understandings** about what they have **learned.**

2. Understanding Conflict & Resolution: Throughout the first two weeks, students read myths in class to determine the types of conflicts that occur (for example, person vs. person, person vs. nature, person vs. self) and how these conflicts are resolved.

3. Word Maps: Students plot word maps to help facilitate their understanding of new vocabulary encountered during the unit. Word maps contain definitions, synonyms, sentences using the word correctly, and illustrations of the word in action.

4. Punctuation Review: Students are presented with a conversation between two mythological characters from which all punctuation has been removed. Students work with a partner to punctuate the conversation correctly and then compare their version with the original.

5. Predictions: Students discuss the name of a mythological character and make predictions about the character in the myth. As they read, students continue to make predictions and confirm or reject those predictions.

6. Analysis: After reading the story of Demeter and Persephone, students determine what naturally occurring phenomena are explained.

7. Descriptive Writing: Students brainstorm words that describe the underworld and then write a descriptive paragraph of what Persephone saw when she was kidnapped by Hades and taken to the underworld.

8. Story Writing and Illustrations: Students examine stories of mythological monsters, then each student creates his or her own mythological monster. Students will illustrate their stories by drawing a picture or making a three-dimensional monster using items from a box of odds and ends and craft supplies.

9. Class Debate: After they read the myth about Prometheus, divide students into two groups. One group will support Prometheus's decision to give man the precious gift of fire. The other group will be support Zeus's decree that man should not be given fire because it would make man too proud and too strong. Students must use evidence and sound reasoning to support their positions.

(Continued on next page)

10. **Collaborative Writing Project:** After reading they myth of Echo and Narcissus, students begin a class book entitled, *Beauty is....* Each member of the class, including the teacher, should make a contribution. For example, someone could write "Beauty is a fiery red sky at sunset." Students illustrate their respective entries. The book will be shared with the principal of the school and excerpts may be shared in the parent newsletter.

11. **Readers Theater:** Students will work in groups to adapt mythological stories into a Readers Theater format and then present their adaptations to the rest of the class.

12. **Personal Essays:** *What if you could do it over?* Like Hercules, we are often ruled by our emotions and sometimes say or do something we regret afterwards. After reading his story, students write a brief account of a similar experience in their own lives, entitled, *If I Could Do It Again*, or *If I Had a Second Chance.*

13. **Researching Idioms:** Students research myth-oriented idioms, such as "Achilles' Heel," and speculate on the meaning of modern-day expressions. Then each student works with a partner to brainstorm a list of other figures of speech that relate to parts of the body, such as "break a leg" and "you are the apple of my eye."

14. **Newspaper Article:** First, students study the differences in an author's style and purpose for newspaper writing vs. fiction. They then identify the basic facts of the Trojan War (who, what, when, where, why, and how) and convert the information into an effective newspaper article. When completed, students compare their news articles.

15. **Review Game:** *What's My Line?* Students generate five sentences about their god or goddess without using the name. Divide students into two teams to play the game. Each player reads his or her sentences, one at a time, to the opposing team to see how few sentences or clues it takes for that team to guess the god. This game will be used at the end of the unit as a review for the unit test.

Culminating Activity

Students demonstrate their new knowledge of mythology by creating scrapbooks that will be displayed in the class museum. Throughout the unit, students will have participated in learning activities from which they may select items they have created to place in their scrapbooks. For example, if a student's assigned goddess is Persephone, that student could include a character map, flowers, a drawing of Persephone, a newspaper article telling of her kidnapping, postcards from the underworld, a mock marriage certificate for Persephone and Hades, or creative diary entries from Persephone's point of view. The teacher should encourage creativity and make it clear that this should be a scrapbook like one a parent might keep for a child with a collection of very important items, not merely a book retelling the story of the child's life. Students should participate in the development of a rubric or scoring guide to evaluate this project *before* they begin their work.

(Continued on next page)

Sample Scoring Guide for Mythology Scrapbook

CRITERIA	4 POINTS	3 POINTS	2 POINTS	1 POINT
Quality of Items in Scrapbook	Items appear to be authentic, and reveal important information about the god/goddess. The items show creativity and are interesting to read.	There are several interesting items that reveal important facts and information about the character.	A few of the items are interesting, but the items do not show very much work or effort.	Items are generic as if they might be included in any character's scrapbook. They are not creative or interesting to read.
Variety of Items (six diary entries is only one item)	11 or more different items are included.	Between eight and ten items are included.	Between five and seven items are included.	Four or fewer items are included.
Neatness and Readability	The items are neatly presented and legible. The pages are attractive and colorful. The scrapbook has the finished or "published" look of something one might purchase.	Most of the items are very neatly presented, but there may be a few pages that are less colorful and lack eye appeal.	A few of the items are not neat, but other items are neat and readable. The book needs more work to make it to "published" status.	The items are messy and difficult to read. It's generally very sloppy or the items are in very rough draft form.
Scrapbook Cover	Cover is intriguing and makes the reader want to open the book and see what's inside. The cover promises that the reader will enjoy the book.	The cover is attractive and interesting. The reader just might pick it up to read.	The cover is neat enough, but there is little that makes the reader want to take a look inside.	The cover is generic or does not convey sufficient information for the reader to know what is inside the book.

(Continued on next page)

Formal Assessments:

1. Newspaper article related to the Trojan War

2. Personal essay: "If I Had a Second Chance"

3. Word maps and vocabulary quizzes

4. Mythological monster story and illustration

5. Character chart of god or goddess

6. Journal entries

7. Descriptive paragraph about the underworld

8. Oral presentation of god or goddess

9. Mythology scrapbook

Informal Assessments:

Teacher's observations of student preparedness, student work samples, and participation in group activities

Daily Lesson Plans

As you know from your student teaching, daily lesson plans keep you on track throughout the class period, because you know before the period begins what you want to accomplish with your students. You probably also learned that flexibility is very important to your success and your sanity every day that you teach. What works well in one class may not be as successful with a different group of students due to so many variables—including the time of day or the weather!

Life would be so easy if there were a perfect lesson plan format that would work like a charm every time. Unfortunately, there isn't one, or if one exists, some teacher is keeping it a big secret. However, the elements of an effective lesson are no secret. For many years, good teachers have been delivering effective lessons. Although there have been many changes in education and the current brain research has shed light on why certain teaching practices work well, one thing remains: Good teaching is good teaching!

Become familiar with the elements of an effective lesson, and you can't go wrong. Within this framework, you will find that you still have so many choices. In some ways, *teaching is like gourmet cooking*. Good cooks never stop perfecting their techniques and expanding their repertoire. The *appetizer*, or **motivational set,** gives students just a taste of what is to come. It prepares the palate for the *main course*, be it **direct instruction, cooperative learning, problem-solving, experimentation,** or other effective teaching methods. Sometimes a lesson will have more than one course, but the transitions are so smooth that the meal flows effortlessly. Finally, there is *dessert*, a chance for our students to savor the experiences by **reflecting on what they have learned**. This "closure" is not only important to students, but it can help inform a teacher's planning, too. Often the closing activity provides informal feedback for the teacher as to whether the lesson objectives have been achieved. Based on the students' responses, a teacher may decide to clarify certain concepts the following day or revisit skills that have not yet been mastered.

To a true connoisseur of restaurant dining, so much value is in the presentation of the meal. I sometimes think that poor planning is fast food at its worst. Imagine a teacher who begins class with these instructions: "Students, you will need to complete these sixteen worksheets today independently, while I catch up on my grading. Don't ask for help, because I do NOT have time to be bothered with your questions."

❖ Tip ❖

Remember to check with your administrator about the required format for lesson plans in your school. He or she may have information pertinent to your building and school district.

Components of an Effective Lesson— A Recipe for Success

As you begin to plan lessons that address student diversity, you may find yourself trying to find new ways of presenting information and searching for learning activities that invite participation instead of stifle student interest. There are certain components that are essential for an effective lesson:

1. Motivational Set

2. Instructional Processes

3. Application and Practice

4. Assessments

5. Reflection and Closure

Within each of the components identified above, you will find hundreds of examples from veteran teachers, many of whom would be flattered if you asked for their ideas! Following is a menu of options from which you may select activities for each of the components of a lesson. It is by no means an exhaustive list. Please add your favorites and continue to borrow more good ideas from your colleagues.

Motivational Set

Capture the attention of your students and connect their prior knowledge with new information that you will present later in the lesson. Always try to establish relevance of the lesson to your students' lives and experiences. The main purpose of the motivational set is to generate interest in your lesson so students will want to learn more about the topic or skill. In a way, you are SELLING the lesson in the first few minutes. When planning how to open a lesson, always ask yourself, *"What will help students buy into the lesson?"* and *"What's in it for them?"*

Here are some examples of effective *openers*:

- ☼ **KWL** ("Know, Wonder, Learn;" see example in the Mythology Unit Plan)

- ☼ **Video Clip** from a news story that relates to course content

- ☼ **Editorial** from a current newspaper related to lesson

- ☼ **Experiment** requiring students to formulate a hypothesis

- ☼ **Journal Writing** with prompts that spark interest in the concept or literature

☼ **Anticipation Guides** (These contain YES/NO/MAYBE SO statements related to the lesson. Students must use prediction skills, their past experiences, and educated guesses to complete the guides.)

☼ **Political Cartoon** related to the topic

Instructional Processes

There are dozens if not hundreds of possibilities from which you may select when planning this phase of your lesson. Key considerations when selecting appropriate instructional processes include the age and maturity of the learners, the students' learning styles, the resources available to you and your school, and the amount of time you can devote to the activity. *Variety* is very important to good teaching. If you want clock-watchers in your classroom, then do the same thing every day. If you want engaged learners who are eager to participate in your lesson, then mix it up a bit when planning activities!

Examples of Instructional Processes:

- Cooperative learning
- Internet research
- Library research
- Interviews
- Reading
- Discussion
- Guest speakers
- Lecture
- Mind maps
- Field trip
- Virtual field trip
- Role play
- Inquiry

Middle-level students enjoy interactive learning experiences that challenge them to think. They want to use their hands, minds, bodies, and voices as they interact meaningfully with knowledge, with resources, and with each other. It is important to think of ways to get students to discuss ideas, ask questions, and work together to solve problems. *Moving Forward with Literature Circles* (Scholastic, 2002) offers some excellent tips for facilitating good class discussions; see page 88.

Tips for Getting Kids Talking in Whole Groups

1. Be quiet! Students can't talk if you do.

2. Avoid evaluative comments such as, "That's good," "That's smart," "That's thinking," and so forth. Praise reinforces your role as a teacher and makes children dependent on you. You want them to know that they have made a good comment because it develops conversation, not because you said it was good. They can't develop sensitivity to that if you chime in with an evaluation.

3. If you must respond, show how their comment develops the conversation. Talk about what a student comment brought to mind. Provide a genuine response, something you would say to another adult in conversation. "I hadn't thought of that before…You know, that makes me think of…I'm not sure I agree, because in my experience…"

4. Model the type of comments you want students to make. Students will copy what you say, so say what you hope they will repeat.

5. Don't stare at the speaker when he or she is speaking to a classmate. Instead, look down or away. If students can see your eyes, they will wait for you to take the lead. But if you focus your attention elsewhere, they are more likely to take the lead themselves. This helps the listeners, too. By looking down or away, you encourage them to look to the speaker, rather than to you, for feedback.

6. If no one talks, look around and try to catch children's eyes. Eye contact often nudges a person into talking.

Reprinted from *Moving Forward with Literature Circles* by Jeni Pollack Day, Dixie Lee Spiegel, Janet McLellan, Valerie B. Brown. New York: Scholastic, 2002

Application and Practice

For many teachers, worksheets were the technique de jour when, as children, they attended grades six through eight. If you happen to be a product of that era of teaching, then you may have empathy for students who are easily bored with busy work. Students do know what "busy work" is, and they will resist it. It would probably benefit middle school students everywhere if all teachers would permanently do away with worksheets and search for more meaningful ways to give students opportunities for application and practice. Consider some of the possibilities for *Application and Practice*:

- Solving real-world problems (using skills and information related to course content)

- Presentations of synthesis of research (on topic related to curriculum)

- Performances and demonstrations of skill mastery

- Readers Theater

- Authentic projects (created for a real purpose—such as a model of a student store to be housed in the cafeteria and run by student council)

- Portfolios of students' best work and works in progress

- Letters to the editor (school newspaper or local newspaper)

- PowerPoint presentations

- Games (designed by students to teach content)

- Television or radio commercial

- Brochures

- Writing and performing a song, rap, or musical

- News report for a local news program

- Television talk shows

- Mock debates and mock trials

- Mock job interviews

- Models

- Mobiles

- Peer teaching

More information about engaging student interest through motivational teaching strategies can be found in Chapter 5.

Assessments

How will you KNOW if your students have mastered the content that you have been teaching them? There are many ways to assess student learning, both formally and informally. As students apply and practice the skills that they have learned, you will need to direct their attention to the quality of their products, performances, and presentations. Many of the projects that students complete are difficult to assess objectively. For example, how do you grade a song that a student has written and performed?

As we move beyond paper and pencil tests, it is essential for students to understand what we expect from them in terms of quality. An effective way for teachers and students to approach the subjective areas of assessment is to incorporate rubrics—scoring guides that identify the criteria to be assessed. Most rubrics assign points on a scale of one to four or five, and utilize descriptors for each score. There are plenty of ready-made rubrics to be found in curriculum materials and on educational websites. However, a more powerful way to help students self-assess and reach for high levels of achievement is to have them help create a rubric for the project they will complete BEFORE they begin working on it. This process gives students ownership of the score and ultimately helps them become more responsible learners who are in control of their own grades.

To the right is an example of a "Four-Point Rubric for Journal Entries," from Laura Robb's book, *35 Must-Have Assessment & Record-Keeping Forms for Reading* published by Scholastic (2001). A simple rubric like this one is a good starting point, and once students become familiar with this form of assessment, they are eager to be involved in creating their own rubrics.

◄ *Assessing students helps you evaluate your teaching and decide what to teach next.*

Four-Point Rubric for Journal Entries

Score 4 Points:

★ Includes several supporting details from the text.

★ Makes personal connections and/or connections to other books.

★ Follows directions carefully.

★ Makes inferences using story details.

Score 3 Points:

★ Includes one to two supporting details.

★ Makes a personal connection.

★ Follows most of the directions.

Score 2 Points:

★ Retells the story.

★ Makes a personal connection.

★ Follows a few directions.

Score 1 Point:

★ Retells the story.

★ Does not follow the directions.

A rubric spells out expectations for students, so they know exactly what they need to do to succeed.

Student's Rubric for Assessing Book Presentations

Note to the teacher:

◉ Before using the following rubric, provide a sign-up list on a chart or chalkboard so that three or four students can sign up each day to make individual five-minute book presentations to the class. Discuss the purpose of book presentations: *Tell just enough about the plot, the characters, and the theme (the author's message) to make others want to read your book and find out how it ends. Give evidence from the story to back up your statements and opinions.*

◉ Show your students the rubric. Answer their questions.

◉ After a student's presentation, in a one-to-one conference, use the rubric to point out what the student could do to improve the next presentation.

◉ Provide photocopies of the rubric so that students can assess each other's presentations.

Key Elements	**3** Excellent	**2** Satisfactory	**1** Needs Improvement
Content	Discusses main ideas, theme, plot and characters; supports opinions with evidence from the story; organizes ideas well.	Describes events and characters, and gives opinions.	Tells a little about a character or an event; rates the books [*good, boring*] with no explanations.
Presentation Skills	Speaks clearly and audibly all of the time.	Speaks clearly and audibly most of the time.	Speaks audibly some of the time.
Presentation Stance	Stands erect; maintains eye contact with audience.	Stands erect and makes eye contact most of the time.	Fidgets; rarely stands erect or makes eye contact.

We must be very clear what it is that we expect of students when we assign projects and presentations, especially when the evaluation of these performances could be very subjective. Take the guesswork out of this process by sharing the rubric with your students before they begin work on the project. Adele Fiderer's book, *40 Rubrics and Checklists to Assess Reading and Writing* (Scholastic, 1999), contains many helpful ready-to-use assessment tools. The rubric at left identifies specific criteria by which students might be evaluated when they do book presentations.

Another good way to identify strengths and weaknesses in student work is to utilize observation checklists. They are quick and easy to use. The important thing to remember when creating an observation checklist is that a student should be aware of what you are looking for in advance. If you want to ensure that students stay on task while they work in cooperative learning groups, let them know ahead of time that you will be using an observation checklist. Show them how you intend to record the frequency of times that group members contribute ideas or do other things that indicate appropriate participation in the activity. Take the mystery out of how you grade students, and you will probably find that they will work hard to meet your expectations, mainly because they know what your expectations are! An example of an observation checklist from Laura Robb's *35 Must-Have Assessment & Record-Keeping Forms for Reading* is shown on the next page.

Remember that students want your feedback more than they want to see a letter grade or number of points. Whatever forms of assessment you use, provide meaningful feedback for students. Even though it is time-consuming for teachers, students need and deserve your comments, praise, and suggestions.

Students enjoy discussing assignment criteria with each other and the teacher.

▼

◄ *This rubric breaks an assignment down into parts, helping students understand what is expected.*

Evaluation of Partner and Group Discussions

Student's Name _____ Observation Date _____

PREPARATION

____ Brought book and materials.

____ Brought response journal.

____ Completed assignment.

____ Contributed to group work plan.

PARTICIPATION

____ Contributes to discussion.

____ Listens without interrupting.

____ Values diverse ideas.

____ Uses text for support.

____ Rereads to point to details.

____ Uses information from other source.

____ Gets involved in discussion.

____ Shares ideas and cooperates.

____ Uses prior knowledge/experiences for support.

____ Addresses ideas presented by peers.

____ Asks meaningful questions.

____ Can help keep discussion flowing.

____ Takes notes at appropriate times.

INTERPRETATION OF MATERIALS

____ Talks about story, problem, or graph.

____ Moves beyond "I like" or "I don't like."

____ Uses pictures and graphs to discover meaning.

____ Makes reasonable predictions.

____ Offers personal connections.

____ Can consider and search out alternate interpretations.

STORY STRUCTURE

____ Can talk meaningfully about plot, setting, characters, time, conflict, mood, dialogue, figurative language.

____ Uses structural elements in discussion.

Additional Notes and Comments:

Reflection and Closure

Sometimes new teachers confuse closure with dismissal. There is a significant difference between effective closure and dismissing students. Both are necessary, yet closure is often forgotten or left out in the interest of time. Teachers need to make an effort to incorporate closure into their lesson plan since closure is what helps students bring the concepts of the lesson together and facilitates understanding. It is a time for students to reflect on what they have learned and, perhaps, to integrate it with what they knew before and what they will learn the next time the class meets. It is the "L" part of a KWL activity—"What I/We Have Learned." Other strategies that get students to reflect on their learning include the following:

- ☼ **"Passport to Leave" or "Ticket Out the Door":** Each student writes down one thing they have learned on a sticky note and shares it with the class before leaving.

- ☼ **Journal writing at the end of the period:** After reading what they wrote in their journals at the opening of the lesson, students see if their opinion or position on the topic has changed or expanded as a result of the class discussion or lesson, and can write about that. Other prompts to use for a closing journal:

    Explain to another student, who may have been absent today, what you learned about _____ .

    Explain how well your group worked together today.

    What thinking strategies did you use today to solve problems?

    What are some real world examples that reflect the same concept that we studied today?

    Write down three questions that you still have about the reading that you did in class.

    Write a four-line poem that summarizes your thoughts on _____ .

- ☼ **Sponge Ball Review:** Distribute two index cards to each student. Divide information from the unit into categories from which students will write review questions (so students don't all write the same questions). Ask students to write one easy (1-point) question on one card and one challenging (2-point) question on the other card. Require students to write the correct answers at the bottom of the cards. Collect and shuffle the cards. Divide the class into two teams to play the game. The teacher tosses a sponge ball to a student, pulls a card, and reads the question. If the student who caught the ball answers correctly, the teacher tosses the ball to another member on the same team. The teacher pulls another card and asks another question. If the student answers incorrectly, the teacher tosses the sponge ball to a member of the other team. Play continues until all questions are answered correctly. Students earn points for their team if they answer the questions correctly.

- ☼ **Finish and review the KWL Chart.**

- ☼ **Preview Coming Attractions:** Introduce a portion of the next day's lesson in the form of a preview or teaser.

- ☼ **3/2/1 Countdown:** Students finish these statements:

  - ◆ 3 facts I learned today…
  - ◆ 2 ways I will use the information/skills I learned today…
  - ◆ 1 question I have…

A Word (or Two) About Transitions

Moving students from one activity to another without losing time can be quite a trick when you are trying to build momentum during a lesson. Posting the agenda in the same place each day is one way to let students know all of the activities that you are expecting to accomplish during the class period. The first rule of thumb is to plan a sequence of activities that naturally leads from one task to another, so that you are building upon previous learning. Then you need to preface the transition with a clear statement that links one activity to the next. For example, "Now that we have brainstormed a list of possible causes for the Revolutionary War, let's read what one of the early settlers wrote in his autobiography." Here are a few tools for making smoother transitions:

- ☼ **Use an advance organizer** that lists activities of the lesson in sequence. Students need to know what is next.

- ☼ **Use a timer or stopwatch.** Make the timer the bad guy so students don't get mad at you when you call time. Let students know before they begin an activity how much time they will have. Say, "You will have about twelve minutes to work on your Mind Maps. When you hear the timer, please look up, and we will move on to the next step." Underestimate the time they will need by a minute or two, so you can add more minutes if necessary rather than let the time drag on if they all finish early.

- ☼ **Use a signal,** such as chimes, a bell, a rain stick, a train whistle, or music, to get their attention when changing activities.

- ☼ **Have students stand, stretch, and then sit down** between activities.

- ☼ **Practice the procedure for transitions**, especially when movement is required.

Lesson Plans for a "Guest Teacher" (Substitute)

The concept of creating smooth transitions can certainly be extended to situations in which your students must make the switch from you to a substitute teacher. If you are absent, you will probably need to arrange for a substitute teacher. Talk with your administrator to find out how you do this in your school district. As you can likely recall from your own school days, there are always some students who hear the word "substitute," and think, "Oh boy, are we going to have fun today!" And if you have ever been a substitute, you know that it is not an easy job. It can be made easier, however, (for the substitute *and* the students) by a classroom teacher who is organized and well prepared. Consider referring to your substitute as a "Guest Teacher." After all, the substitute brings expertise with him or her and is actually a guest in your classroom. Remind students that a "Guest Teacher" is there to teach, not babysit!

Taking care of the logistics involved in having a guest teacher can be very time consuming if you do not have **procedures** in place. Once your students know exactly what you expect and they have practiced the procedures so that they become routines, their behavior will probably be fairly good when there is a substitute.

To make the day go smoothly, it is very important that you prepare lesson plans that are simple and organized so they can be easily understood by the substitute teacher. Use the same format each time you need a substitute; this will make your task of organizing for a substitute's arrival easier. Your regular substitute (if you are lucky enough to find one) will also benefit from the consistency of the format. Keep several blank copies of a Daily Lesson Plan format at home in case you need to have someone deliver plans to your school.

Always keep **backup lesson plans** on hand for those true emergencies when you cannot formulate a daily plan. The backup plan should be an enrichment activity rather than an activity based on a specific unit or concept idea and may include appropriate group activities, games, or independent reading assignments that can be easily facilitated by a substitute teacher and completed by the students. The location of these plans should be noted in your substitute folder with the stipulation that *they are to be used only if regular plans are not available.*

Tips for Preparing for a "Guest Teacher" (Substitute)

I. When you are explaining your classroom rules at the beginning of the year, tell students how you expect them to behave when there is a substitute in your classroom.

2. If possible, review your classroom rules and procedures the day before you are going to be absent. Remind students about the consequences for not following the rules, and that you hope they will treat the substitute as a "Guest Teacher." If you let them know that you think they are capable of earning an excellent report from the substitute, chances are they will try to meet your expectations.

3. Long before you are absent, write down your classroom procedures and routines so that a substitute would not have to guess how you do things in your classroom. The more information you give your substitute, the better able he or she will be to manage your classroom efficiently.

4. Leave detailed lesson plans that are simple enough to follow, but not so simple that the students race through the activities. *Over plan* so the substitute is not in the position of having to tap dance or discipline students who have nothing to do!

5. Try to keep the momentum of your class going. If students see the assignment as busy work, they may rebel or refuse to do it, since they think that it won't count toward their grade anyway. Remember, not all substitute teachers are as skilled in your content area as you are. Plan activities that students can manage to do without a lot of direct instruction from the teacher. Review activities, writing assignments, and problem-solving tasks work well on days when you are absent.

6. List names of helpful students and helpful teachers on whom the substitute can call if necessary.

7. When you return, follow through if there were any disciplinary actions taken by the substitute. Acknowledge students who were helpful, and let the class know that you appreciate their cooperation. Sometimes small treats (candy or stickers) are in order if students have been especially good!

8. If, when you return, you are unhappy with the job that the substitute has done, do not criticize the substitute in front of your students. It sends the message that substitutes aren't professionals and should not be respected. Follow up by letting your administrator know about your concerns. Sometimes, substitutes need additional training or reminders about following teachers' lesson plans and classroom procedures.

Information for the Guest Teacher

Teacher's Name: _____ School: _____

Teaching Schedule:

PERIOD	TIME	SUBJECT	ROOM #
1			
2			
3			
4			
5			
6			

Helpful teachers should a question or concern arise:

TEACHER   **ROOM #**

_____   _____

_____   _____

_____   _____

PERIOD	NAMES OF HELPFUL STUDENTS
1	
2	
3	
4	
5	
6	

(Continued on next page)

Location of Instructional Resources:

Daily Lesson Plans: _____

Emergency Lesson Plans: _____

Seating Charts: _____

Attendance Records: _____

Teacher's Editions: _____

Curriculum Guides: _____

Staff Handbook: _____

Technology/Equipment: _____

Paper and Other Supplies: _____

Special Materials: _____

Location of Items for Emergencies:

First Aid Kit: _____

Key to Fire Alarm: _____

Shelter in Place Supplies: _____

Health Office Passes: _____

Classroom Management Information:

1. Procedures for opening of class _____

_____

2. Procedure for sharpening pencils _____

_____

(Continued on next page)

The New Teacher's Complete Sourcebook: Middle School   Scholastic Professional Books

3. Procedure for acquiring and using restroom passes _____

_____

4. Procedure for clean-up and class dismissal_____

_____

5. Procedure for fire drill _____

_____

6. Procedure for shelter in place drill _____

_____

7. Procedure for calling the office to summon help _____

_____

8. Other classroom procedures _____

_____

Classroom Rules: _____

_____

Consequences for not following classroom rules: _____

_____

Location of teacher mailbox: _____

Location of staff lounge: _____

Location of photocopy machine: _____

Location of telephone:_____

Course Expectations Sheets

Tip

Place all the parent signature forms in a three-ring binder, organized by class period and alphabetized. Then, when you need to make parent telephone calls, you will have all of the information at hand. Simply use the back of the sheet for documenting any communication you have with parents (date, time of call, person you spoke with, topic of praise or concern, further action to be taken, etc.). You can bring this three-ring binder and your grade book with you when you attend parent conferences. You will feel confident when you are prepared.

Tip

Most administrators require that you submit your course expectations sheets to them for approval prior to having them copied and distributed to students. The earlier you prepare them, the better chance you will have of getting them approved and printed in time to distribute them during the first week of school. You may want to wait until the end of the first week to go over the course expectations sheets, since you may be getting additional new students the first few days of school. (But don't put off teaching and practicing classroom procedures; begin that process on the first day.)

The purpose of a Course Expectations sheet is to provide information to students and their parents/guardians regarding the content of your class and your academic and behavioral expectations. For your consideration, I have included a model sheet that may be helpful, but check with your supervising administrator, as he/she may have information to share with you that is pertinent to your school. You may need to meet with your team members to coordinate your behavioral expectations, classroom rules, and certain procedures. The more consistent that you and your team teachers are with procedures and rules, the more likely that your students will follow the procedures and rules in all of their classes.

Obtaining parent information (i.e., name, telephone number) can be rather time consuming in a large school, so you may want to use a format for your parent signature sheet that requests their address and telephone numbers (see sample on next page).

Remember that your students have five other teachers who will also be introducing their course expectations. Get your students' attention by having them do a scavenger hunt or some other activity with your course expectations sheets. You can make up 20 questions, and students can work with a partner to locate the information and write down the correct answers. Possible questions:

1. How do you obtain make-up work after an absence?

2. What is the lowest possible percentage that you may earn and still get an "A"?

3. What is the exact title of the textbook that we will use in this class?

4. How much homework can you expect to have in this class?

5. What are the required sections in your class notebook?

Require your students to keep a copy of the course expectations in their notebooks.

School Name
Course Expectations
Teacher Name
Course Title

I. COURSE DESCRIPTION—

Include applicable information from the current CCSD course curriculum guide.

   A. Course Scope and Objectives

   B. Textbook(s) and/or Materials

II. COURSE OUTLINE

   A. Outline of course—units of study and approximate timelines

   B. Major projects/papers and approximate due dates/schedule

III. HOURS OF AVAILABILITY

Indicate daily times when you will be available to assist students and explain how students may schedule an appointment for special assistance. Also explain how students will be notified when parent conferences, club activities, or other functions may alter your schedule and/or availability to students.

IV. GRADING POLICY

   A. Grading Scale: (example: 90% = A, 80% = B)

   B. Description of Grading Practices

      1. The value and approximate percentages of the total grade that homework, quizzes, tests, major reports, projects, and other assignments will have for the grading period

      2. Attendance impact on grade, if any

      3. Classroom participation impact on grade, if any

(Continued on next page)

4. **Notebooks**—their purpose, and how and when evaluated (All classes should expect students to maintain some type of notebook.)

5. **Homework**—nature and type of homework; how often a student can expect to have homework; and how much (quantity and time) they should expect

C. Standards of Preparation—All classes include a statement regarding the impact of spelling, grammar, neatness, and adherence to standards on grade received.

D. Basis for Semester Grade—how the semester grade is calculated (example: 40% first quarter, 40% second quarter, 20% semester exam)

E. Make-Up Procedures—suggested entries include:

1. After an absence, the students must initiate a request for make-up homework (or retrieve it from the appropriate files/folders) within two school days directly after the student's return from the absence.

2. How unexcused absences are handled regarding make-up work

3. Procedure for turning in make-up work

4. Procedures for making up tests, quizzes, and other in-class work

V. CLASSROOM BEHAVIOR EXPECTATIONS

A. Classroom rules

B. Discipline plan explanation and procedures

C. Suggested information to include, stated briefly:

1. Tardy (for example, 1/2 hour late = one absence)

2. Corridor and restroom passes

3. Policy on food, drinks, gum, and candy in the classroom

4. Behavior expected during class assignments and activities

5. Behavior expected at the beginning and end of class

6. Care of school and personal property

7. Other items unique to your classroom and program

(Continued on next page)

VI. CITIZENSHIP

Identify how citizenship grade will be determined (Excellent, Satisfactory, Unsatisfactory).

VII. SIGNATURES REQUIRED FOR STUDENTS AND PARENT/GUARDIAN

Include required signatures on a separate sheet (see sample). This enables students to retain your expectations sheet and return only that portion that indicates that they and their parent/guardian have received your course expectations.

VIII. OTHER PERTINENT ITEMS unique to your classroom.

IX. STATEMENT THAT THE COURSE EXPECTATIONS ARE SUBJECT TO CHANGE.

Example: *Students and parents will receive an addendum to these course expectations if the instructor deems it necessary to make any modifications during the school year.*

Attach Parent Signature Form (page 106) to Course Expectations Sheets

Parent Signature Form
for Course Expectations

PLEASE PRINT!

Name of student: _____
First   Last

Period _____1 _____2 _____3 _____4 _____5 _____6

Name(s) of Parents/Guardians: (First and last names)

_____

_____

Mailing Address: _____

_____

Parent/Guardian's Home Phone: _____

Parent/Guardian's Work Phone: _____

Parent/Guardian's E-mail Address: _____

Best time to call and where? _____

I have read the course expectations and understand that I must take responsibility for my academic advancement, as well as my classroom behavior.

X_____
Student Signature   Date

I have read and discussed with my son/daughter the Course Expectations for this course.

X_____
Parent/Guardian Signature   Date

Parents/Guardians: Please feel free to add any comments or call with any questions.

106

The New Teacher's Complete Sourcebook: Middle School   Scholastic Professional Books

CHAPTER 5

Powerful Teaching Strategies

for Motivating Students

Throughout your teacher preparation courses, you undoubtedly received information about teaching methods; and if you were very lucky, your university professors modeled effective teaching strategies. Unfortunately, for many new teachers, their university experience consisted of a traditional lesson format: read, listen to lectures, and then take a test. You will very quickly learn, if you haven't already guessed, that read/lecture/test is one of the *least* effective ways to teach a diverse population of middle-level students.

Fifteen years ago, when I was finishing my teaching degree, I was not given any information about brain research and its implications on how students learn. In fact, 90% of the books on brain research have been written only within the last ten years. The information delivered by pioneers in the field, such as Marian Diamond, R. & G. Caine, Pat Wolfe, David Sousa, and Eric Jensen, has awakened new interest in how teachers might provide optimal learning experiences for students.

Experts in the field of education are cautious about jumping too quickly on a proverbial bandwagon, but the findings from the field of neuroscience validate what good teachers have been doing for years. We have long known that learners must connect new information to prior knowledge, but now we know why. It is not my purpose to explain the scientific changes that occur in the brain every time a person learns. Rather, I strongly recommend that all new (and experienced) teachers become informed about current brain research and its implications on student learning. (For a list of excellent resources on brain research, see the bibliography provided at the end of this chapter.) What I would like to share with you are some key principles that will help guide you as you select powerful strategies to engage your students in meaningful learning.

What Brain Research Tells Us About Intrinsic Motivation and Learning

In his book, *Brain-Based Learning*, Eric Jensen provides a list of seventeen conditions that elicit intrinsic motivation in students. When I read his work, I was encouraged by his premise that the brain is hard-wired to want to learn. In fact, the primary purpose of the human brain is to survive. Simply put, one cannot survive without learning. (When I think of some of the most at-risk students I have taught, their ability to *survive* surpasses many college-educated people that I know.)

There are not enough gold stars, stickers, or Tootsie Rolls® in the world to keep rewarding students for every little bit of progress that they make on their journey through school. If you have doubts about the long-term effectiveness of extrinsic rewards, then you are in good company. As teachers, we need to find ways to get students to value learning for itself, not because we will reward them with certificates, trophies, or behavior bucks. We want them to show up, become engaged in the lesson, and actually *learn* something.

Of Eric Jensen's list of seventeen conditions, I have experimented extensively with the following five, using strategies and structures in the classroom that foster these conditions:

- ✿ Meeting students' needs and goals
- ✿ Incorporating multiple intelligences
- ✿ Engaging appropriate emotions
- ✿ Supporting students' sense of curiosity
- ✿ Celebrating student learning

I've included my interpretation and application of these five conditions, which I believe are vital to fostering intrinsic motivation in the classroom. There are many other conditions that elicit intrinsic motivation, but these five are within our influence and can make a huge difference in getting middle school students to buy into learning our curriculum.

Meeting Students' Needs and Goals

Humans learn what they need to know in order to survive. Therefore, a key motivator for students today is *relevance*. When students can make connections between their own lives and the content that we wish them to learn, they are more willing to engage in the learning activities that we present. Hang up a sign in your classroom that asks, *When will I use what your are teaching me today?* (And make a point of answering that question from time to time, especially if you suspect student interest is lagging.) Students have a need and a right to know the answer to this question.

As educators, we are responsible for meeting our students' educational needs. You will find that some of your students are very needy. They need your attention, your interest, your patience, and on some days, your last nerve. As we search for ways to make our curriculum relevant to our students, we must be on the lookout for high-interest literature—books, poems, articles, and information that will help them connect with the topics that we teach.

20 Worthwhile Core Books That Can Reach All Readers

Baby, by Patricia MacLachan. Bantam, Doubleday, Dell, 1984.

The Book of Three by Lloyd Alexander. Bantam, Doubleday, Dell, 1984.

Boy: Tales of Childhood by Roald Dahl. Farrar, Straus & Giroux, 1984.

The Children's Story by James Clavell. Bantam, Doubleday, Dell, 1963.

The Dark Stairs by Betsy Byars. Puffin, 1997.

Dear Mr. Henshaw by Beverly Cleary. Morrow, 1983.

The Face in the Frost by John Bellairs. Macmillan Children's Books, 1991.

The Friendship by Mildred D. Taylor. Dial, 1987.

The Green Book by Jill Paton Walsh. Farrar, Straus & Giroux, 1986.

Hiroshima by Laurence Yep. Scholastic, 1995.

The Language of Goldfish by Zibby O'Neal. Puffin, 1990.

The Midwife's Apprentice by Karen Cushman. Houghton Mifflin, 1995.

Nightjohn by Gary Paulsen. Doubleday, 1993.

The Outsiders by S.E. Hinton. Viking Press, 1967.

The Pinballs by Betsy Byars. HarperCollins, 1977.

Sadako and the Thousand Paper Cranes by Eleanor Coerr. Dell, 1979.

Shades of Gray by Carolyn Reeder. Simon & Schuster, 1989.

Shiloh by Phyllis Reynolds Naylor. Atheneum, 1991.

Stone Fox by John Reynolds Gardiner. HarperCollins, 1988.

What Jamie Saw by Carolyn Coman. Puffin, 1997.

The Window by Michael Dorris. Hyperion, 1997.

Reprinted from *Teaching Reading in Middle School* by Laura Robb. New York: Scholastic, 2000

Check with your school librarian to obtain additional high-interest book titles that pertain to your course content.

If you don't know what your students' goals are, then ASK them! They will be surprised, if not shocked, that you are consulting them about what their expectations are for taking your course. It is not enough merely to ask for a few students to raise their hands and tell you what they want to learn in your class this year. Make it real—and personal—by asking them to enter into a contract with you. Keep the contract simple, and make sure that each student writes at least two goals. A third goal may be one upon which the whole class has reached a consensus such as *Have fun while learning*. Even with this simple goal, you will have achieved a major victory. Combine learning and fun, and you will have activated another condition for intrinsic motivation: **engaging appropriate emotions** to enhance learning. The next step is to identify what both parties must do in order to reach the goals.

Contract for Academic Success

Student: _____ Teacher: _____

Course: _____ Date: _____

It is the intent of this agreement that both parties will cooperate in working toward
the mutual goals listed herein:

Student's Goals:

1. _____

2. _____

3. _____

Teacher's Goals:

1. _____

2. _____

3. _____

Student's statement of what he/she intends to do to work toward achieving these goals:

_____

_____

Teacher's statement of what he/she intends to do to work toward achieving these goals:

_____

_____

This contract will be reviewed at the midpoint and end of the semester to record progress toward meeting the
goals of both parties.

Record of Progress toward Achieving Goals

CHECK POINT	RECORD OF GOAL ACHIEVEMENT
End of First Quarter	
End of Second Quarter	
End of Third Quarter	
End of Fourth Quarter	

_____   _____

Student's Signature   Teacher's Signature

The New Teacher's Complete Sourcebook: Middle School Scholastic Professional Books

Characteristics of the Middle-Level Student

To meet your students' needs and goals, it is helpful to recognize some of the physical, emotional, social, and intellectual characteristics of middle-level students. These characteristics have implications on how you might plan instruction that addresses the wide developmental range that is common in a middle-level classroom. After spending a few months with students ages 11 to 15, you will soon be able to list some of these developmental characteristics, even though there is great variability among students within each grade level.

In the area of *physical development*, many young adolescents experience rapid, irregular physical growth, which accounts for the disparity in size and physical maturity that you see when you look at a classroom full of students. They often experience restlessness and fatigue due to hormonal changes, and *they need physical activity* because of increased energy. When we expect our students to sit down, be quiet, and hold still, we are often asking them to do what is painfully different from what they actually need.

Incorporate *purposeful movement* during your instruction, so students can meet their need to MOVE around and can get oxygen back to their brains. Between learning activities, invite your students to stand, stretch, and sway to eight or sixteen counts of an energizing song. Students can be taught how to transform the physical arrangement of the classroom quickly by moving their desks to form small groups when it is appropriate, or to help you collect and distribute materials in the classroom. Incorporating movement into the lesson in purposeful ways can prove motivating to middle-level students.

In the area of *emotional and social development*, young adolescents often experience mood swings. That accounts for the hysterical laughter you may hear one moment and the crocodile tears you see the next moment from the same student! Middle-school students are often concerned about peer acceptance, yet they think that they are the only ones who feel a certain way or experience certain problems. Many tend to be self-conscious and sensitive to personal criticism. Consequently, we sometimes see middle-level students resist high-risk learning activities, such as individual presentations to the class. We can make them more comfortable by assigning group projects and performances and by providing opportunities to practice their speaking skills in small groups. Since middle-level students have a strong need to belong to a group, team-building activities (such as those mentioned in Chapter 3) are essential to set the stage for building healthy peer relationships in your classroom.

In the area of *intellectual development*, young adolescents are in a transition period from concrete thinking to abstract thinking. They prefer *active* rather than *passive* learning experiences, even though they often have a very short attention span. Learning activities that are *hands-on, application-oriented*, and *relevant to their lives* will be those that are favored by middle-level students.

Incorporating Multiple Intelligences

Teach students that there are multiple definitions of intelligence
(verbal-linguistic, logical-mathematical, visual-spatial, musical-
rhythmic, bodily-kinesthetic, interpersonal, intrapersonal, naturalist). Share
Howard Gardner's research on multiple intelligences. With this information,
students can discover *how* they are smart in school and in life. Traditionally,
schools have focused exclusively on the verbal/linguistic and
logical/mathematical intelligences. However, many students excel in other
areas. Their strengths can be magnified in your classroom and used to bridge
into the curricular areas that you teach. If you want your students to come
alive, use multiple intelligences as you present new information and as you
assess student learning. Kristen Nicholson-Nelson's "Eight Ways of Being
Smart," from her book, *Developing Students' Multiple Intelligences* (Scholastic,
1998) is a good way to introduce the concept and to help build students'
self-esteem and confidence about their individual learning styles; see chart
on page 114.

▲

*Students focus their attention and energy on tasks that address their talents
and strengths.*

☀ Eight Ways of Being Smart ☼

Intelligence Area	Is Strong In:	Likes To:	Learns Best Through:	Famous Examples:
Verbal-Linguistic	reading, writing, telling stories, memorizing dates, thinking in words	read, write, tell stories, talk, memorize, work at puzzles	reading, hearing and seeing words, speaking, writing, discussing, and debating	T.S. Eliot, Maya Angelou, Virginia Woolf, Abraham Lincoln
Mathematical-Logical	math, reasoning, logic, problem-solving, patterns	solve problems, question, work with numbers, experiment	working with patterns and relationships, classifying, categorizing, working with the abstract	Albert Einstein, John Dewey, Susanne Langer
Visual-Spatial	reading, maps, charts, drawing, mazes, puzzles, imagining things, visualization	design, draw, build, create, daydream, look at pictures	working with pictures and colors, visualizing, using the mind's eye, drawing	Pablo Picasso, Frank Lloyd Wright, Georgia O'Keefe, Bobby Fischer
Bodily-Kinesthetic	athletics, dancing, acting, crafts, using tools	move around, touch and talk, use body language	touching, moving, processing knowledge through bodily sensations	Charlie Chaplin, Martina Navratilova, Magic Johnson
Musical-Rhythmic	singing, picking up sounds, remembering melodies, rhythms	sing, hum, play an instrument, listen to music	rhythm, melody, singing, listening to music and melodies	Leonard Bernstein, Wolfgang Amadeus Mozart, Ella Fitzgerald
Interpersonal	understanding people, leading, organizing, communicating, resolving conflicts, selling	have friends, talk to people, join groups	sharing, comparing, relating, interviewing, cooperating	Mahatma Gandhi, Ronald Reagan, Mother Theresa
Intrapersonal	understanding self, recognizing strengths and weaknesses, setting goals	work alone, reflect, pursue interests	working alone, doing self-paced projects, having space, reflecting	Eleanor Roosevelt, Sigmund Freud, Thomas Merton
Naturalist	understanding nature, making distinctions, identifying flora and fauna	be involved with nature, make distinctions	working in nature, exploring living things, learning about plants and natural events	John Muir, Charles Darwin, Luther Burbank

Allow Students to Illustrate Vocabulary Terms

To a **visual learner**, a picture is worth a thousand words. To make vocabulary study meaningful and to help students learn the meanings of new words and keep them in their long-term memory, try having students create pictograms. A pictogram is a graphic representation of a word, wherein the word becomes an illustration of the word's meaning. Some words work better than others do, but students are very creative when it comes to making words into pictures. See examples on page 116.

Students sketch pictures to illustrate new vocabulary words.

Representing a word graphically helps students remember its meaning.

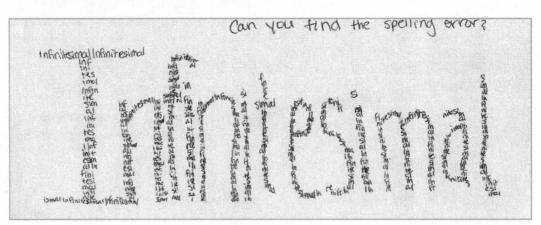

In addition to traditional vocabulary exercises, ask students to illustrate their vocabulary terms by drawing a picture of the word used in context. They will need to understand whether the word is a noun, adjective, adverb, or verb in order to illustrate the concept. They may create a cartoon or comic strip in which several vocabulary words from the unit are shown in action. The students' illustrations will become cues to help them remember what the words really mean. Illustrating vocabulary is a strategy that empowers students to "own" the words instead of passively copying definitions from the dictionary.

Review Important Concepts through Songfests

A fun and engaging way to incorporate **musical/rhythmic intelligence** into your instruction is to have students rewrite lyrics to popular songs. It is fairly easy, once students get the hang of it. This activity can be used at the end of a unit to review facts and information or to present research information that students have gathered and synthesized for a team project. You may also invite students to put their vocabulary words to music to help them memorize difficult terms. Below is a sample assignment used during a unit on tall tales, by Victoria Yeomanson, English Teacher.

Students who possess musical/rhythmic intelligence often enjoy performing lyrics they've written to review or present information.

# Songfest: Group Assignment

Directions:

Choose any song which has a recognizable melody (for example, the theme to *The Brady Bunch* or *Gilligan's Island*) Do not choose something that only one person in your group knows—popular, well-known songs work best for this assignment. Your song must be about either Pecos Bill or John Henry. When you have written the song, rehearse it together. It isn't necessary to memorize it, but you will all be performing it for the class, so the smoother the performance, the better! You will not be graded on the quality of your voices, but you will be graded on completion, originality, following directions, and total group involvement. You can earn extra points by adding movement. You will lose points if you fool around. After presenting the songs to the class, each group must turn in a paper to me. The paper should include your lyrics, the name of the song you took the tune from, and the first and last names of all members of your group. You may NOT talk or practice when other groups are presenting.

Time to work: 40 minutes

Points: 25

Students are motivated when they are provided with opportunities to choose activities that appeal to the strongest of their multiple intelligences. They will also benefit from stretching their talents a bit to try new ways of accessing information. Give students options when they are preparing to deliver their research findings; often they will discover new and exciting ways to present their work, ways that will connect with other learners in the classroom. Instead of always requiring a written research report, offer other ways for students to show what they know. Why not allow students to create a dance, a game, or a public service announcement as a way to share the information they have gathered and synthesized?

As you plan your units, brainstorm activities that allow students to access and utilize their multiple intelligences. Use a planning web like the one on page 120 to ensure that you consider many different possibilities for teaching and assessing the content within your unit plan.

◀ *An eighth-grade student opens her speech on Charles Darwin by stating, "Imagine that you are an educated religious scholar and that your life's work will challenge the notion of human existence."*

Sample Web for Teaching Persuasive Writing

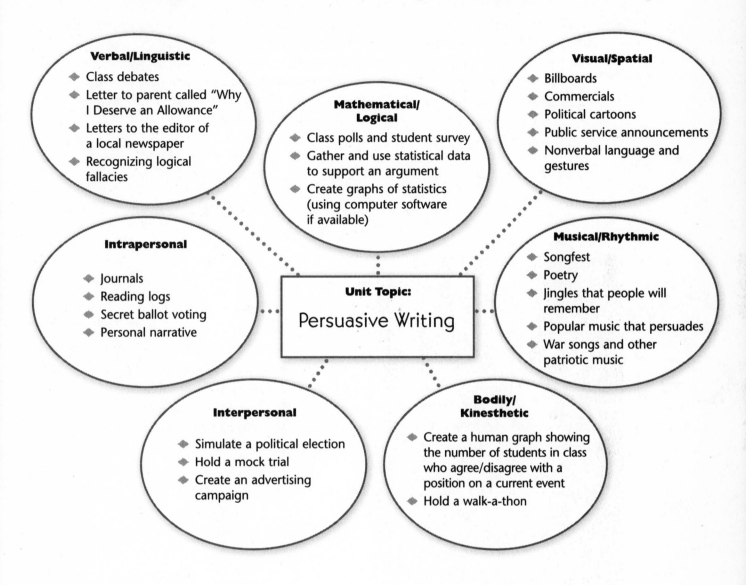

Verbal/Linguistic
- Class debates
- Letter to parent called "Why I Deserve an Allowance"
- Letters to the editor of a local newspaper
- Recognizing logical fallacies

Mathematical/Logical
- Class polls and student survey
- Gather and use statistical data to support an argument
- Create graphs of statistics (using computer software if available)

Visual/Spatial
- Billboards
- Commercials
- Political cartoons
- Public service announcements
- Nonverbal language and gestures

Intrapersonal
- Journals
- Reading logs
- Secret ballot voting
- Personal narrative

Unit Topic:
Persuasive Writing

Musical/Rhythmic
- Songfest
- Poetry
- Jingles that people will remember
- Popular music that persuades
- War songs and other patriotic music

Interpersonal
- Simulate a political election
- Hold a mock trial
- Create an advertising campaign

Bodily/Kinesthetic
- Create a human graph showing the number of students in class who agree/disagree with a position on a current event
- Hold a walk-a-thon

There's also another category that you may want to work into your activities: environmentalist or "naturalist."

Naturalist

- Organize a recycling program for the school
- Student presentations on energy conservation
- Raise funds to buy a tree to plant on campus

Planning Web for Targeting Multiple Intelligences

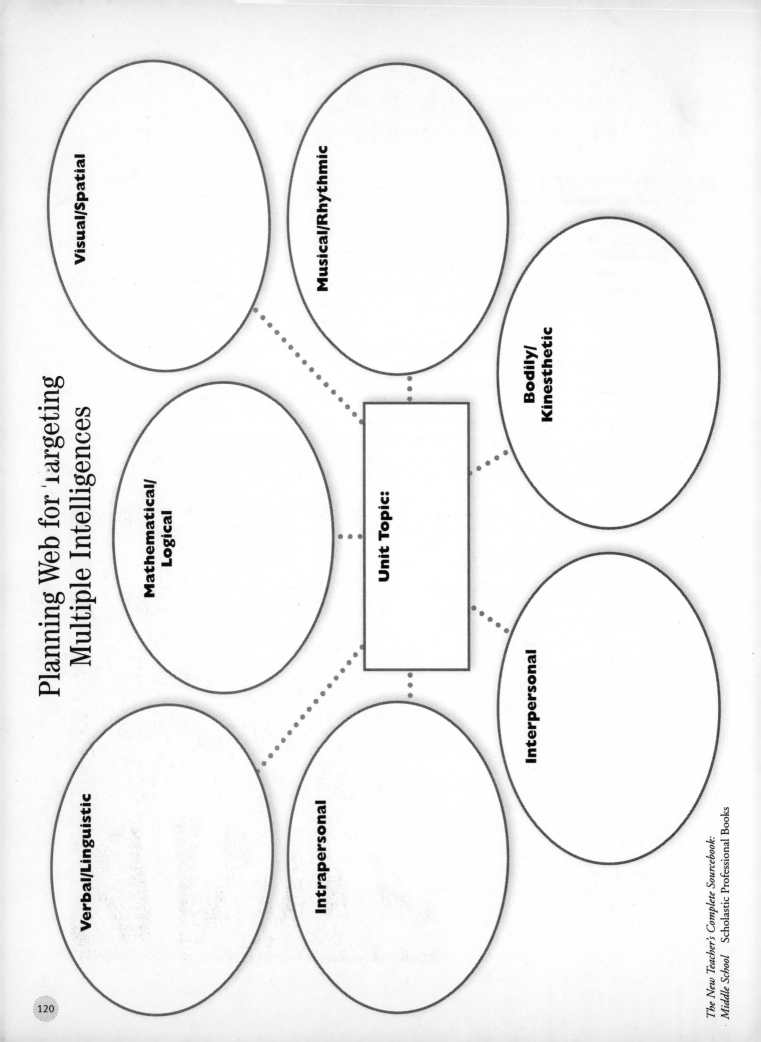

Visual/Spatial

Musical/Rhythmic

Bodily/Kinesthetic

Mathematical/Logical

Unit Topic:

Interpersonal

Verbal/Linguistic

Intrapersonal

The New Teacher's Complete Sourcebook:
Middle School   Scholastic Professional Books

Engaging Appropriate Emotions to Enhance Learning

We know from brain research that *students are likely to retain information that was learned when their emotions were engaged.* For proof of the power of emotions, just try to remember your first grade experiences. Chances are the event or situation that you clearly recall is one packed with emotion—either positive or negative. There is an optimal amount of emotion necessary for learning—too little and students' minds will likely be elsewhere; too much and you may have an unpleasant or explosive situation. For example, the brain automatically moves the body to flight or fight in response to extreme stress or threat, so it makes sense to create and maintain a classroom environment where students feel it is safe to experience and express emotions.

An important skill that all middle school students can—and should—develop is the capacity for using tact to good effect when disagreeing and debating controversial issues. Middle-level students need opportunities to disagree and debate authority, but they do not automatically know how to do this without offending others. Provide a list of ground rules for your students before discussing emotionally charged topics. For example:

1. Preface your opinions with the words, "I think…"

2. Attack ideas, not people, in our classroom.

3. Do not interrupt another person who is speaking.

4. Wait to be acknowledged by the discussion leader before speaking.

5. Show respect for all members of our class, even if you disagree with their ideas.

A sixth-grade student proudly shares the final product of his "How to Make Popcorn Balls" expository writing project. ▶

Ten Ideas for Engaging Appropriate Emotions in the Classroom

1. Use **current events** to introduce curricular topics.

2. Share **compelling stories** from history, young adult literature, or picture books related to course content.

Books That Hook Readers

- *Boy: Tales of Childhood* by Roald Dahl. Puffin, 1984.

- *The Cartoonist* by Betsy Byars. Puffin, 1987.

- *Dear Mr. Henshaw* by Beverly Cleary. Morrow, 1983.

- *I'm Not Who You Think I Am* by Peg Kehret. Dutton, 1999.

- *Journey* by Patricia MacLachlan. Delacore, 1991

- *Knights of the Kitchen Table* by Jon Sceiszka. Viking, 1991.

- *The Language of Goldfish* by Zibby O'Neal. Puffin, 1990.

- *The Music of Dolphins* by Karen Hesse. Scholastic, 1996.

- *The Not-so-Jolly Roger* by Jon Sceiszka. Viking, 1991

- *Protecting Marie* by Kevin Henkes. Greenwillow, 1995.

- *Strider* by Beverly Cleary, Morrow. 1991.

- *Then Again, Maybe I Won't* by Judy Blume. Dell, 1971.

- *Your Mother Was a Neanderthal* by Jon Sceiszka. Viking, 1993.

- *2095* by Jon Sceiszka, Viking. 1995.

Reprinted from *Teaching Reading in Middle School* by Laura Robb. New York: Scholastic, 2000

3. Hold **debates**, **mock trials**, and facilitate **lively class discussions**. Check out *50 Debate Prompts for Kids* by Patrick Daley and Alexander Pavlenka (Scholastic, 2001) for some terrific ideas.

4. Model the joy of learning. Share great books that you are reading with your students. Show them that adults can be lifelong learners and that you learn things from teaching them that help you to be a better teacher.

5. Utilize prompts in **journal writing** that require students to relate course content or curricular issues to their own lives.

6. Think of ways to **simulate real-world** events that pertain to your course curriculum. Some examples include a stock market game, escape from slavery using the underground railroad, census, elections, book publishing, advertising campaign, passing a bill in Congress, public service announcements for social causes, documentaries, and Olympics.

7. Offer students **choices** (within reason) when it comes to selecting topics for research. Negotiate certain aspects of instruction so students feel compelled to become involved in making decisions that are important to them.

8. Infuse your instruction with **relevance**. The more timely the topics you teach, the more interested students will be. Think about what is going on in the world today and more specifically in the world of adolescents. How can you connect your course content with what is important to students?

9. Create opportunities for students to have **authentic audiences**; they need good reasons for being creative and for utilizing their academic skills. For example, students can write letters to real people, conveying their beliefs and understanding of important issues. Possible audiences include the local newspaper editor, school superintendent, President of the United States, career professionals who are experts in their field, parents, and local politicians. Students may write to these people to express opinions, seek advice, ask for changes, express appreciation, suggest solutions, or to obtain information.

10. Provide opportunities for **service learning**. As you develop unit plans, consider how students might become involved in giving something back to the community. Most students want to help others in meaningful ways. Many times in my teaching career, students have generated ideas for community service projects related to our topics of study. For example, during our study of the book *Maniac Magee*, by Jerry Spinelli, one class decided to serve lunch at a local soup kitchen for homeless people in our city. Another group of students decided to make sack lunches for the homeless in our community. Five hundred peanut butter and jelly sandwiches were assembled in my classroom one Saturday morning. The students were exhilarated when we finished cleaning up and delivered the lunches to the nearby shelter.

Service learning projects, like preparing food for local soup kitchens, are a great way to involve students in meaningful learning.

Other service-learning projects that have been highly successful include a shoes and socks drive for our state orphanage, a Readers Theater for children at a neighboring elementary school, and Valentines that students made and delivered to a nursing home in our community. Recently, Janice Jensen, a teacher at my school, spearheaded a "Red, White, and Blue Snow Cone Sale" to raise money for the victims of the New York City tragedy that occurred on September 11, 2001. Students in her class created a huge poster, displayed in our cafeteria, depicting a graph of the money they have raised thus far. So far, students have sold over 700 snow cones, at one dollar apiece. Every day they race to the cafeteria to sell the snow cones during lunchtime. They will not stop until they reach their goal of $2,001. Talk about motivation!

Eliciting Curiosity to Capture and Sustain Attention

Curiosity is such an obvious condition for intrinsic motivation that we often overlook it when we are planning instruction. Think about situations in your own life when you have been motivated to learn more about a topic because you were curious. In the classroom, the trick is to introduce new material or information in ways that quickly capture the attention of your students and leave them wanting to know more. In a way, our opening strategies are like bait on a hook. We are fishing for their interest. Be creative! Try something unusual or puzzling to stimulate curiosity when you begin a lesson or launch a new unit. Also, remember to use the teachable moment in the middle of a lesson when a student asks a question that begs to be researched. It may be the perfect moment, for instance, to invite a student to do a quick keyword search using online resources. Students' questions are excellent clues as to what makes them curious.

Possibilities for Stimulating Curiosity in the Classroom

1. Use **conundrums**, **puzzles**, and **mysteries** related to course content. Unlike dry textbook material, mysteries get reluctant students interested in reading, thinking, and writing. Launch a lesson using a puzzling scenario to pull students into the content and nudge them into higher levels of thinking. For ideas on using mysteries in the classroom, visit this web site: **http://www.midgefrazel.net/mystclas.html**.

2. Show **video clips** (NOT entire pieces) of news magazine stories that teach critical information. Ask students to predict the outcome of these investigations and to offer evidence and support for their assertions.

3. Use **demonstrations** and **experiments** to hook learners before teaching the underlying principles that follow. Use the simple P.O.E. strategy: students *predict, observe,* and *explain* phenomena that you demonstrate. For example, in a science class, students could observe socks dried with a fabric softener sheet and socks dried without. The teacher might ask students to predict what will happen when he pulls the socks apart. Students record their predictions, observations, and explanations of the phenomenon.

4. Preview **coming attractions** at the end of the class period, so students want to come back the next day and learn more—a sort of "tune in tomorrow for…" hook.

5. Provide a **scavenger hunt** for students in lieu of a traditional worksheet or questions at the end of the chapter. Scramble the order of questions so students have to use chapter headings, the index, and the table of contents to find answers to questions. Include questions that require students to read graphs, tables, and captions of pictures in the text. Divide students into two teams and give half the questions to each team. Allow students to work together to find answers. At the conclusion of the activity, students from both teams share their answers with the whole class.

6. Stimulate students' curiosity by giving them an **anticipation guide** to be used at the beginning of a lesson or new unit. Formulate statements that activate students' emotions and prior knowledge. The statements can be facts or they can be opinions to which students may agree or disagree. Anticipation guides are NOT tests, but they will give you insight into how students think and feel about a topic related to your curriculum. The advantage to this strategy is that students will be immediately engaged in the content and curious about what will come next in your lesson. You may invite students to compare their responses with a learning partner and then discuss the statements as a class.

◀ *Curious students stay engaged.*

Sample Anticipation Guide
for *Zlata's Diary*

Directions:

Before we begin reading the book, please read each statement. In the "anticipation" column write "**YES**" by those statements with which you agree and "**NO**" by those with which you disagree. Remember to write your reason for agreeing or disagreeing.

ANTICIPATION   **STATEMENT**

_____   **1.** Parents are always stronger than children.

Reason:

_____   **2.** No wars have been fought in Europe since World War II.

Reason:

_____   **3.** It is possible for children to feel suicidal.

Reason:

_____   **4.** Nobody would want to read the diary of a young girl.

Reason:

_____   **5.** If a group of people is being bombed and killed by another group of people, the United States should get involved and help the first group.

Reason:

❋ Tip ❋

Learn more about planning effective cooperative learning for your students by reading *Cooperative Learning: Where Heart Meets Mind*, by Barrie Bennett, Carol Rolheiser-Bennet and Laurie Stevahn (Bothell, Washington: Professional Development Associates, 1991).

Encouraging Social Interaction Through Cooperative Learning Structures

What teacher of adolescents doesn't know that students today are highly social beings? *Students want to talk*—but often when *we* want them to be quiet and listen. What we may forget is that for many students, **social interaction** (talking) is a way of learning. When students verbally rehearse information that you have taught them, they are forming neural connections that will help them put the new information into long-term memory. Talking with their peers about the content of your course is a powerful way for them to reinforce what they have learned. Instead of constantly saying "Stop Talking!" say, "Turn to your partner and recap what your have just learned about _____. You have 2 minutes. Go!"

◀ *Learning partners discuss their photographs for the "Amazing Invention" writing project.*

Quick Ways to Incorporate Social Interaction Effectively in the Classroom

1. **Learning Partners** are very important for getting students to rehearse what they have learned and to explore their understanding of content. But sometimes, students will slip into socializing about unrelated topics if you do not give them a specific amount of time (two and a half minutes, for example) and a specific prompt for discussion. Use a kitchen timer to keep students (and yourself) aware of the time constraints. Give students a little less time than you think they will actually need. It is easier to add more seconds if necessary than to let the minutes drag on with students getting off task.

2. **Paired Verbal Fluency** is a cooperative structure in which partners are asked to summarize their knowledge or ideas about a topic or issue. All partners stand and face each other. They decide who is Person A and who is Person B before you begin the activity. When the teacher says "*Go,*" Person A speaks for thirty seconds about the topic. Person B listens and does not interrupt Person A. When the teacher says, "Switch," then Person B speaks for thirty seconds about the topic. *The catch is that Person B cannot repeat anything that Person A has already said.* Person A must listen without interrupting while Person B speaks. Then the teacher says, "Time!" and all students stop talking and remain standing. The teacher can process this activity by asking, "What did you learn from your partner that you had not thought of or that you had forgotten?" This activity works well as an energizer and requires students to rehearse the information that they are learning. Model this activity for your students before they try it with a partner.

3. **Reciprocal Teaching** provides students with an opportunity to engage in elaborate rehearsal of material they are learning, to process information in depth. The saying, "The best way to learn something is to teach it," is so true. Teaching a concept or skill you've learned to someone else requires a fairly high level of understanding. Periodically during direct instruction or lecture, stop and have students pair up, one partner being "A" and the other "B." During the first round, student A teaches student B the content that has just been covered. Later the roles are reversed and B teaches A. It's fast and it's fun, and best of all, it makes students active learners, rather than passive participants.

4. Group students randomly for short cooperative learning activities. Sometimes you may ask students to work together on a task that will only last for one class period. There is no reason to spend hours deliberating over which students should work together for short learning activities. On the contrary, part of your goal is to help students develop their social skills by working with students they may not ordinarily choose as partners. Frame each brief cooperative activity by explaining that when people put their heads together to solve problems and accomplish tasks, they can be more effective than when they work alone. You may quickly group students by using playing cards like "Go Fish" so students work with their "school," or type, of fish. You could also use any group of items that can be sorted by color, shape, or type. Hand an item to each student as they enter the class, then reseat students once it is time to work cooperatively in groups.

Students work cooperatively to arrange countries in correct formation for a map project.

Celebrating Student Learning

Do you remember the last time you really celebrated an occasion? For most people, celebrations stimulate the release of endorphins (the brain chemicals are partying!). When we **celebrate student achievement and learning**, we are acknowledging our students in very positive ways. Try to focus on intrinsic motivation, by refraining from giving tangible rewards like stickers and prizes. Celebrations can be very simple (spontaneous applause) or more elaborate (a publishing party). Develop traditions in your class for students to celebrate achievement, whether it be class pictures, high fives, a hall of fame, or a standing ovation.

Celebratory Traditions for a Community of Learners

1. **Class Photos:** Assemble students for a class photograph or take pictures of students working in class throughout the school year. One student told a new teacher how much he liked seeing himself in the class picture she displayed on the bulletin board. He told her that there are no pictures of him in his home. Young adolescents have a strong need to belong. Class pictures show them that they do have a special place in the school community and in your heart.

Middle school students love to see photos of themselves displayed in the classroom. ▼

2. Top Ten Lists: Invite students to compile lists on various topics relating to your curriculum in ascending order of importance. If you allow students to work in small groups to generate their ideas, the lists will be more creative and interesting, plus students must come to a consensus about which items are most important. Peer edit for content, spelling, grammar and capitalization. Encourage students to illustrate their lists for visual appeal. You may display their Top Ten lists in class during the last few weeks or days of the term. You may want to display one or two different lists on a daily or weekly basis to increase student anticipation of what's coming up next. Suggestions for Top Ten lists:

- Top Ten Ways to Handle Tests/Assignments/Projects
- Top Ten Things I Learned in This Unit
- Top Ten Things I Learned This Year
- Top Ten Tips for Next Year's Incoming Class

3. A to Z Activity: Using each letter of the alphabet as a starting point, students can describe the year or a unit of study. One letter can be assigned to each student, groups can be responsible for a few letters, or the entire class can brainstorm possibilities and come to a consensus. Possible prompts for this activity may include the following:

- The best thing about this year has been…
- Environmental science is…
- Learning to speak Spanish is like…
- One thing from this class I'll never forget is…

4. Blast from the Past: Put a wrap on the end of the semester or school year by inviting your students to write a letter to themselves to be mailed to them in five years. Phil Paulucci, a veteran teacher at Southern Nevada Vocational and Technical Center, began this tradition in this first year of teaching. As an end-of-the-year activity, he asks his students to write letters to themselves that describe their lives, friends, and goals for the future. I was very fortunate to have Mr. Paulucci as my cooperating teacher many years ago when I was student teaching. I remember that many students included pictures, love notes from their boyfriends or girlfriends, and other memorabilia. Students put their letters in self-addressed stamped envelopes (allowing for inevitable postage increases). At the end of each school year, Mr. Paulucci mails the letters written five years earlier. He often receives phone calls and letters from former students when they get their "blast from the past." It's a great activity for bringing closure to the end of another year.

5. Fortune Teller Activity: You will need balloons, small slips of paper, and some celebration music for this activity. Explain to your students that you would like them to take a few minutes to reflect on the key concepts and skills that they have learned in your class this year. Then, distribute small pieces of paper (1-inch by 3-inch) and ask students to write a fortune or wish for someone in the class that in some way captures something essential that has been learned. Provide an example so they understand that this activity is like writing a fortune in a cookie, but that they will be putting the fortunes in balloons. An example of a fortune for an English class could be *May you remember to release your fears and do a quick write when you have writer's block.*

Have students roll up the paper and place it in a balloon. Ask them to blow up the balloon, tie it, and hold it until everyone is ready. Play 60 seconds of upbeat music. "Celebration" by Kool and the Gang and "Celebrate" by Madonna are good choices. While the music is played, students toss the balloons in the air, and keep them up until the music stops. Then each student grabs a balloon of a different color than the one he or she had originally. At your signal ("1, 2, 3!"), students pop the balloons and read their fortunes to themselves. Finally, students form a large circle, and each student reads his or her fortune aloud. This activity is fun and only takes about 15 minutes. More important, you will find that students listen carefully to the fortunes.

Impact of Teacher Expectations on Student Achievement

Our expectations of our students are communicated in so many ways. When we smile, nod, make eye contact, and pay attention to our students' needs, we are telegraphing our belief that they are important and capable. We show them that we trust their judgement when we allow them to make choices about what they learn and how they might best learn it. If we offer very little variety and limited stimulation in our instruction, our students may think that we don't believe they can handle difficult curriculum. Their doubts can become self-fulfilling prophesies, and our work in the classroom can become tedious, if not boring.

Experiment with conditions that foster intrinsic motivation, and you and your students will benefit greatly. You will find that exciting lessons promote student attention and decrease discipline problems. The time and effort that you put into making sure that students' needs are met through social interaction and challenging learning activities is well worth it. Try something new! What do you have to lose?

Bibliography of Resources

Caine, Geoffrey and Renate Caine (Eds). *Making Connections: Teaching and the Human Brain*. Menlo Park, CA: Addison-Wesley, 1994.

Daley, Patrick and Alexander Pavlenka. *50 Debate Prompts for Kids*. New York, NY: Scholastic, 2001.

Diamond, Marion and Janet Hopson. *Magic Trees of the Mind*. New York, NY: Dutton, 1998.

Jensen, Eric. *Brain-Based Learning*. San Diego, CA: The Brain Store, 2000.

Nicholson-Nelson, Kristen. *Developing Students' Multiple Intelligences*. New York, NY: Scholastic, 1998.

Parry, Terence and Gayle Gregory. *Designing Brain Compatible Learning*. Arlington Heights, IL: SkyLight, 1998.

Sousa, David A. *How the Brain Learns,* Second Edition. Thousand Oaks, CA: Corwin Press, Inc., 2001.

Sylwester, Robert. *A Celebration of Neurons*. Alexandria, VA: ASCD, 1995.

CHAPTER 6

Whose Grade Is It?

Measuring Student Achievement

Next to planning, grading student work is probably the most time-consuming aspect of teaching. Yet assessment is essential, if we are to hold students accountable for their learning. Measuring student achievement also serves another vital purpose. The information that we gather when we grade student work helps us to know if we have done *our job* in teaching the skills and information that we are assessing. There have been occasions when I have found that my students performed poorly on a test, not because of their lack of preparation, but because I had not taught the material in the most brain-compatible way (for more information about brain-compatible teaching, please refer to Chapter 5: "Powerful Teaching Strategies for Motivating Diverse Learners").

Many issues related to assessment and grading are covered extensively in teacher preparation programs. However, there are practical components of grading that most teachers learn on the job.

These components are addressed in this chapter as a "heads-up" for new teachers. Consider their implications and always ask, "What is my goal in grading student work?" Most teachers are not out to get students, trying to catch them doing the wrong thing as often as possible. Still, some students feel that way, year after year, as they experience ongoing failure in school. Make a conscious decision to look for what students do well when you sit down to grade a batch of essays, tests, or other assignments. It will help you keep your perspective, and your positive comments will encourage students to strive for higher levels of achievement.

In some ways, your students' grades are your grades. You are the one who taught them the information and skills being assessed. Their success is your success. Of course, we want our students to assume responsibility for their performance in school, but we also want them to know that we are rooting for them. We communicate our desire for them to reach their potential by the manner in which we invite them to participate in evaluation practices. It is just amazing how honest and accurate students are when they self-evaluate. Often they are harder on themselves than we are. While they can become adept at assigning an accurate grade for their homework, essays, and projects, they have the tools to identify quality in their own work. We can help them develop a language for talking about quality work by using rubrics and checklists. Then they will know how well they have performed on an academic task *and* what they can do to improve.

Using Pretests and Assessments to Inform Your Planning

In the beginning of the school year, you need to find out what your students know. This information will help you in planning how you will structure your semester and which areas you may need to target for review. Use **pretests** and collect **work samples** to determine at what level to begin your instruction. Many publishers of textbooks include ready-to-use pretests in their teacher editions, or you may check with your department coordinator or grade-level leader to obtain ideas for creating your own pretests. A KWL chart (see page 79) is another effective way to find out what students' previous knowledge is on a given topic.

In addition to measuring the abilities of individual students and the overall class level, pretests also help students by giving them some idea of the focus of the course. A pretest clearly illustrates to students that while there are concepts they need to learn, they already know something about several of the content areas.

As depicted below, the teaching process requires *ongoing assessment of student learning* in order to be effective.

* Tip *

When preparing the pretest, include an opportunity for students to list:

- what they think their strengths and weaknesses are in this subject area

- what they like the most and least about this subject

- what they hope to gain from this course, or what their goals are

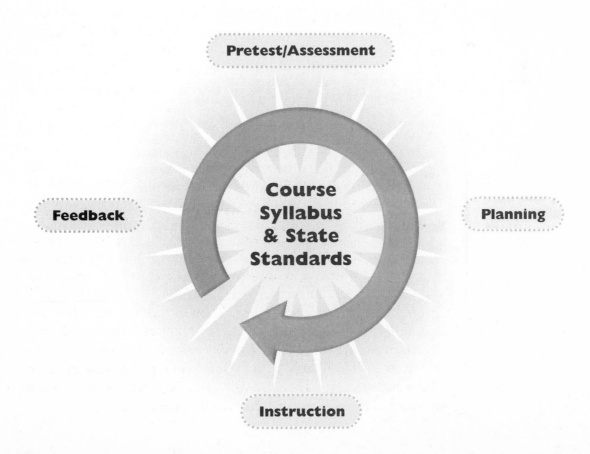

Pretest/Assessment

Feedback

Course Syllabus & State Standards

Planning

Instruction

Decisions that Impact Your Grading System

You must determine your grading system before you begin evaluating student work, and you will need to convey your grading system to students and parents in your course expectations sheet or in a letter sent home the first week of school. You may choose to utilize a point system, or you may use percentages or letter grades. Whatever you decide, make sure that you are fair and consistent as you grade and record student work. Decide in advance, for example, how heavily each aspect of student work is weighted for the final quarter and semester grades.

For example, will homework count as much as tests? How will you give students credit for participation in class discussions and cooperative learning activities? Talk with other teachers in your department to find best practices for fair and effective grading. Once you determine how much homework, quizzes, tests, and projects will count, you can easily enter this information into a computerized grade program, which will automatically weight the scores. Electronic grading programs will also save you hours of time when you need to average student grades. Check with your school administrator to find out if your school has a site license for grading software. If you do not have access to computer grade-book software, then you will need to calculate the weight of each category of work that your students produce.

Considerations for Establishing Fair and Effective Grading Practices

☼ When calculating quarter or semester grades, you may want to place more emphasis on daily work, as it provides a better overall representation of a student's efforts than does one test given on a particular day. Seek out your supervising administrator if you need assistance developing your formula.

☼ A true point system provides the most accurate method of formulating grades and also simplifies your work when adding extra credit points or participation points to a student's overall grades.

☼ If you will be rounding up a student's grade, you may want to use .5 as a marker.

✧ Consider setting a limit on the total amount of extra credit points, if any, that a student may earn in your class. Sometimes students will slack off and do as little as possible, thinking that at the last minute they can bring up their grade by earning lots of extra credit.

✧ Decide whether you will accept papers with no names. Think about the message that you want to send to your students about responsibility. Do you have the time or should you make the time to hunt for students to sign their papers? You may decide to require that students' names be on their papers in order for them to receive credit for their work. If so, be sure to post this rule of "NO NAME, NO CREDIT" in full view of all students and discuss it with them at the beginning of the course.

✧ Always tell students when you will collect an assignment and follow through on that. If you do not, you may lose your students' trust; those who work hard to complete their assignments on time will think it is unfair and may begin to come to class unprepared.

✧ Make it a habit to collect homework at the beginning of the class period on the day that it is due. Once you have collected the homework, staple the stack of papers together to prevent students from slipping in a late assignment after working on the homework during class.

✧ Require your students to keep track of their own grades by utilizing student grade record sheets (see sample on next page). Student grade sheets prevent students from taking up your time to ask for updates of their averages. They also help students identify missing assignments and help parents stay informed of their child's progress.

Student Grade Record

Name: _____ Quarter: _____

Class: _____ Teacher: _____

Date	Assignment Title	Points Possible	Points Earned	Percent	Grade

The New Teacher's Complete Sourcebook: Middle School   Scholastic Professional Books

Seven Questions to Consider When Planning Assessments

1. What evidence can your students give you to show what they have learned?

2. How will you know if your students can apply the concepts they have learned?

3. At what level of Bloom's Taxonomy (knowledge, comprehension, application, analysis, synthesis, evaluation) are you testing your students?

4. Have you given your students time and direction in practicing the processes that you are assessing?

5. Did you break projects into smaller parts and evaluate the parts?

6. How will you make your students aware of your expectations and criteria prior to the assessment?

7. How will you provide opportunities to incorporate multiple intelligences and varying learning styles within the assessment? (See Chapter 5: "Powerful Teaching Strategies for Motivating Students.")

Developing Authentic Assessments

It would by unfair to test students at the level of application, analysis, synthesis, or evaluation if you have not provided opportunities for students to wrestle with higher-order thinking operations during instruction. Therefore, strive to incorporate all levels of Bloom's Taxonomy as you develop effective questions for class discussion and as you plan learning experiences. For example, to show their understanding of the concept of *survival*, students could make backpacks for survival in a specific biome. To show their understanding of *weight and equations*, students could build a math bridge. To demonstrate their understanding of probability, students could design carnival games. Complex learning experiences require students to do far more than rote memorization. They must use the information they

Bloom's Taxonomy

In 1956 Benjamin Bloom, a professor at the University of Chicago, shared his now-famous "Taxonomy of Educational Objectives." Bloom identified six levels of cognitive complexity that have been used over the past four decades to make sure that instruction stimulates and develops students' higher-order thinking skills. The levels are:

- ☼ **Knowledge:** Rote memory skills (facts, terms, procedures, classification systems)

- ☼ **Comprehension:** The ability to translate, paraphrase, interpret, or extrapolate material

- ☼ **Application:** The capacity to transfer knowledge from one setting to another

- ☼ **Analysis:** The ability to discover and differentiate the component parts of a larger whole

- ☼ **Synthesis:** The ability to weave component parts into a coherent whole

- ☼ **Evaluation:** The ability to judge the value or use of information using a set of standards

As cited in *Developing Students' Multiple Intelligences* by Kristen Nicholson-Nelson (Scholastic, 1998)

have learned and apply the skills and operations necessary to solve problems.

Young adolescents enjoy creating projects that utilize their academic strengths. Through Howard Gardner's research on Multiple Intelligences, we know that students learn differently and that they show their understanding in different ways. According to Wiggins and McTigue (as quoted in Glenda Ward Beamon's *Teaching with the Adolescent in Mind* [SkyLight Professional Development, 2001]), when adolescents really understand a concept, they should be able to do the following:

1. **Explain it.** How can you explain the impact of this war on the country's economy? What accounts for this conclusion? What is implied in this action?

2. **Interpret it.** What makes sense about this play's ending? How does this style of writing reflect the political climate of the period? How does this historical event illustrate a pattern in human behavior?

3. **Apply it.** How can this knowledge of statistics be used in a different situation? In what real-world context is this economic principle applicable?

4. **Take a perspective on it.** What are the two sides of this political debate? From whose viewpoint is this article written? What are the strengths and weaknesses of this rationale?

5. **Show empathy about it.** How would you feel if you were in an immigrant's shoes? How would these changes impact the way of life for this culture? How are these decisions detrimental to these peoples' well-being?

6. **Gain self-knowledge through it.** What prejudices am I recognizing in myself? How might I formulate questions better? Where was my thinking faulty? How can I use these suggestions constructively?

(from *Teaching with the Adolescent in Mind* by Glenda Ward Beamon)

Consider the levels of Bloom's Taxonomy, Gardner's Multiple Intelligences, and Wiggins's suggestions for getting students to interact more fully with information, concepts, and skill development. You will need to be flexible in offering a variety of tasks to students throughout the year so all students have opportunities to showcase their talents and develop their intellectual strengths.

Assessments that offer choice and flexibility to students foster a sense of ownership, which contributes to high levels of achievement.

Your written comments on a paper mean more than a grade at the top. Be positive. You can be *positively critical*! Here are ten examples of encouraging comments on students' essays:

◆ Your first sentence grabbed my attention right away!

◆ You support your argument with very strong evidence.

◆ Your explanation is clear.

◆ I am interested in knowing more about…

◆ I can actually "see" what you describe.

◆ You helped me to consider it from another point of view!

◆ Please expand on this idea. I can't wait to hear more!

◆ I am convinced!

◆ Your thoughts flow smoothly from one paragraph to the next.

◆ Good for you! You used one of our vocabulary words here.

Tips on Grading Papers

When correcting papers, use green ink instead of red. The color red is often associated with negative feelings and may have an impact on the students' perception of your feedback.

Develop a code to use in the margins of papers to signal errors in paragraph style or grammar. Students learn more when they must locate an error themselves than if you circle their misspelled words or insert correct punctuation for them. Be sure to write the code for the error on the line in which the error occurs. Make a copy of your code and distribute it to each student. Post one on a bulletin board, as well.

Sample Code

sp	spelling error
p	punctuation error
ss	sentence structure (confusing, poorly constructed)
wc	word choice (incorrect use of a word)
ro	run-on sentence
fr	fragment (incomplete sentence)
sm	see me (this correction requires further instruction; see teacher for discussion)

Strive to return graded student papers within 2-3 days. Research shows that the more time that elapses between completion of a task and receiving feedback on that task, the less meaningful the feedback becomes.

Never write only the points or grade on a paper. Students will remember your comments longer than any score or grade. Remember that written feedback gives specific direction for improvement; scores and grades do not.

Before returning graded assignments, give a brief overview of the positive aspects of the assignment as well as areas that need improvement. This gives students a better idea of what you were thinking and looking for when grading their papers.

Grading papers as a class (with the exception of tests and subjective essays) can save hours of time that will be better spent planning and developing your lessons. It helps students learn more because it allows them to review the material another time. Students are also able to receive prompt feedback. Make sure that students' names are not visible on the papers that will be graded by peers. Instead, use student numbers to protect the privacy of your students. Having students sign the papers they correct helps make them more responsible. Let students know that you will be checking the papers to ensure that they are being graded accurately.

"Yes, it counts!"
Homework and Other Assignments

What will you say when students ask, "Does this assignment count?" It's a loaded question. If you say, "Not really, it's just practice to prepare you for the test, which *does* count," some students will not make their best effort. They may interpret your well-meant response to mean, "No, this does not count, so don't worry about doing it."

Just like a good coach, teachers know that practice is crucial to skill development. In fact, everything that we ask our students to do "counts." If it doesn't, then why are we doing it? Even if the activity will not be "graded," students need to know that their full participation is expected. Many teachers give participation points each day to account for the hands-on activities and cooperative group work required. You may use your seating chart to put checkmarks next to students' names as they take part in class activities. You may have students self-evaluate their participation as part of their grade on group projects and other informal activities that you routinely do in class; see sample evaluation form on page 147.

This self-evaluation tool is very generic, but you can make the instrument more specific by creating a rubric (together with your students) to identify the criteria by which the project will be evaluated. To empower students, the rubric must be understood prior to completing the assignment.

◀ *Inviting students to evaluate their own performance in group activities helps them see that their contributions "count!"*

General Guidelines for Evaluating Individual Projects

☼ Criteria for evaluation should be established before projects are started.

☼ Involving students in creating the rubric will increase their motivation.

☼ Evaluate the *process* of project development as well as the finished *product*.

☼ Limit the criteria to no more than six when beginning to work with rubrics.

☼ Give students very clear examples of what each score on the scale represents.

Project Self-Evaluation

Name: _____

Date: _____

My overall contribution to the group project deserves the following grade:

A　　**B**　　**C**　　**D**　　**F**

I have earned this grade for the following reasons:

_____

_____

_____

One thing I would do differently next time to improve:

_____

_____

_____

Project Scoring Guide

Name: _____ Period: _____

Project Title: _____ Date: _____

Rate each of the elements of your project using this rating scale:

3 = Excellent   2 = Good   1 = Fair   0 = No Evidence

CRITERIA	TEACHER'S SCORE	STUDENT'S SCORE
1. Choice of topic	_____	_____
2. Quality of research	_____	_____
3. Organization	_____	_____
4. Knowledge of topic	_____	_____
5. Imagination or creativity	_____	_____
6. Neatness and readability	_____	_____
7. Use of graphics, color, or other visuals	_____	_____
TOTAL POINTS	_____	_____

What do you think was the best thing about your project?

Student _____

Teacher _____

What do you think might be improved on your project?

Student _____

Teacher _____

Student's Comments: _____

_____

Teacher's Comments: _____

_____

The New Teacher's Complete Sourcebook: Middle School   Scholastic Professional Books

Rubric for Cooperative Learning Group Performance

Directions: Review the steps you completed to plan, prepare, and deliver your presentation. Complete each of the statements below to analyze how well the members of your group worked together. Select the most appropriate rating for each area and be able to defend your decision to other members of the group.

Rating Scale: **3 = Super**   **2 = Satisfactory**   **1 = Needs Improvement**

_____ **1.** Each member of our group handled his or her group role appropriately.

_____ **2.** Each member of our group took turns listening to one another's ideas.

_____ **3.** Each member of our group actively engaged in the assigned learning task.

_____ **4.** Each member of our group applied his or her conflict resolution skills when appropriate.

_____ **5.** Each member of our group showed respect for one another.

_____ **6.** Each member of our group made a major contribution to the overall performance.

_____ **7.** Each member of our group displayed a sense of humor.

_____ **8.** Each member of our group seemed to enjoy the assignment.

Summary:

If I were the teacher or the audience of this performance, I would give our group a(n)_____

(letter grade) because _____

_____

_____

_____

_____

_____

_____

Name _____ Date _____

From: *Making Portfolios, Products, and Performances Meaningful and Manageable for Students and Teachers*, by Imogene Forte and Sandra Schurr, Incentive Publications, 1995.

Connecting With Parents for Positive Support

Communicating with parents can be very beneficial to your success in reaching the students in your classroom. It is good to begin with the premise that every parent wants what is best for his or her child. That way, when you deal with difficult parents or with parents whose children are difficult, you will remember that parents want to help their child be successful, too. Therefore, parents are on your team! If you keep parents in the communication loop, they are in a better position to encourage and support their child in being successful in your class. Everyone wins when parents are partners with teachers in educating their children.

Keeping parents informed starts at the beginning of the school year. Don't wait until students are experiencing problems to make contact with parents. Give them good news first, BEFORE any problems arise. If you want parents to be supportive, then you must invite them to be part of the educational process. They don't need to be sitting in your classroom to help their children, but they do need to know what you expect from their children—both academically and behaviorally. Again, most parents really want the best possible education for their children. Get them on your team by connecting with them through positive communication, and they will reinforce your behavioral and academic goals.

Positive News Postcards and Telephone Calls

Send parents good news postcards recognizing the positive achievements or good behavior of their son or daughter. Typically, parents only hear from the school when their children are in trouble. Set aside ten minutes each week to send two or three notes to different parents.

And don't just acknowledge students who are getting A's. Recognize the student who has made significant *improvement* or one who did an outstanding job on one assignment. You will be surprised at how much parents appreciate hearing good news about their child's progress. Most

---

Good News! ⭐

To: _____
(Parent's/Guardian's Name)

From: _____
(Teacher's Name)

_____
(Name of School)

Just a quick note to tell you how pleased I am that:

_____

_____

_____

_____   _____
(Signed)   (Date)

Parents love hearing good things about their children. A form like this makes it easy to send that news home.

schools have pre-printed postcards that are available for this purpose, or you can create your own. To save time and to give a student positive recognition, you might have the student address the card to his or her parent or guardian. That way the student knows that good news is on its way home.

You can also call parents or e-mail them to communicate some good news about their child's accomplishments. It may catch them off guard, but they will most likely be very appreciative. Plus, *you* will feel great when you share good news about your students!

Reminders for Parent Communications

☼ **Begin and end conferences with a positive statement about the student, no matter what the purpose of the conference.** If you begin with a critical or accusatory tone, the parent may become defensive and not "hear" your concern for their child.

☼ **Keep a record of the parents with whom you've had conferences in your plan book or on your calendar.** Many teachers keep a running log of all parent contacts on the back of the student information cards (or sheets) that they collected on the first day. Write down the date, name of the person you spoke with, the reason for the conference (or telephone call), and the response from the parent.

☼ **Maintain a professional demeanor throughout all parent conferences.**

☼ **Avoid educational jargon when you are speaking with parents.** Use language that parents understand.

☼ **Be sure parents know that you care and have a sincere interest in their child's personal and educational growth.**

☼ **If a conference does not go smoothly, schedule another meeting with the parent or parents.** Ask the school's counselor or your supervising administrator to attend this second conference.

☼ **Always carefully proofread all written correspondence that you are sending to parents.** Spelling and grammar errors are unacceptable. Remember that you are representing yourself, your school, and the teaching profession.

Ten Tips for Conducting Successful Parent Conferences

1. Before the conference, plan what you hope to accomplish. What information do you want to share with the parent? What problems need solving? Do not overwhelm the parent. Identify no more than two or three concerns to be addressed.

2. Make sure that you are prepared to begin the conference by saying something positive about the student. It will put the parents at ease and let them know that you are not picking on their child, but that you value their son or daughter.

3. If possible, clarify ahead of time who will be attending the conference and the relationship to the child. Also verify from the school records the person's name. Do *not* assume their surname will be the same as the student's.

4. Come prepared with the following items:

 ◆ Grade book (student's up-to-date average)

 ◆ Course Expectations sheet (with parent's signature)

 ◆ Sample of student's work (if possible)

 ◆ Record of behaviors of concern

 ◆ Computer printout of student's grade (if available)

 ◆ List of missing assignments (if necessary)

5. Maintain a sense of professionalism. Avoid getting emotional in discussing problems you may be having with the student. Remember that your goal is to enlist the parent's cooperation in resolving any difficulties the student may be having in your class. Allow parents time to express their own thoughts and concerns.

6. Try to offer two or three specific suggestions for the parent(s) to implement at home that might help the student.

7. End the conference in a hopeful tone. Summarize the main points discussed and any steps to be taken to resolve identified problems.

8. Invite parents to contact you with any future concerns about their child's progress in your class.

9. Thank the parent(s) for coming to the conference.

10. Follow up with notes in the student's planner, and a telephone call or e-mail message to the parents letting them know how their child has progressed since the conference.

The OREO® Effect

"**P**reparation for parent communication always begins with documentation. Whether the situation is about grades or a discipline problem, I always bring materials with me to the conference. Once I am ready with the appropriate documentation, I use the same formula for any conference: 'The Oreo Effect.' Begin positively, get to the center issue, and end with a positive resolution or proposal without going on the defensive. 'The Oreo Effect' hasn't failed me yet; it allows me to stay professional and empathetic."

—*Heidi Olive, social studies teacher*

Keeping Parents Informed

Consider sending home a brief letter to parents at the beginning of the year to introduce yourself, your philosophy, and your expectations regarding assignments, homework, and general student behavior in the classroom. Include a shopping list of student materials that you recommend (such as notebook, paper, and colored pencils). Let parents know where and when you may be reached to answer questions and/or receive their comments. Have your administrator approve the letter before you send it to parents.

Sometimes you just need to let a parent know that a student has been unprepared for class. You may not need to hold a conference, but you do need to inform the parent so that the problem does not become chronic. Some teachers create a quarter-page notice called a "H.A.M." (Homework Assignment Missing) or an "Unprepared Notice." If you print these on NCR paper, you will be able to keep a record of how many times a student and parent have been informed of the problem.

❋ Tip ❋

Keep parents informed about their child's progress by using the student's agenda or planner whenever possible, especially if a parent has expressed a concern such as, "How do I know if my child has homework?"

H.A.M. (Homework Assignment Missing)

Name: _____ Date: _____

Dear Parent:

Today I was missing the following homework assignment:

_____

The reason I did not turn in my homework is: _____

_____

My plan for completing this work is: _____

To contact my teacher, please call _____ , or e-mail

_____.

_____   _____

STUDENT'S SIGNATURE   TEACHER'S SIGNATURE

Unprepared Notice

As a concerned parent, you will want to stay informed about your child's progress at school.

This notice is to inform you that_____

was unprepared on his/her _____
(subject)

assignment on _____.
(date)

Please sign and return this notice. You may reach me at _____ ,

if you have any questions or comments.

Sincerely,_____
(Teacher)

Parent Comments:

_____

Parent Signature _____

Student Progress Reports

Throughout the school year, you may receive requests for Student Progress Reports from parents, school counselors, special education caseworkers, and coaches. If your grade book is kept up to date, it shouldn't be too difficult for you to complete the progress report and return it in a timely manner. Be sure that you respond to the request before the deadline because there may be important decisions to be made based on the student's academic standing.

You can create your own Student Progress Report to use for those times when you need to inform parents about an area of concern. Include a space for a parent's signature and require that students return the form to you after their parents have read and signed the form. The form created by Nancy Schneider, a social studies teacher, is a good example (see next page). Nancy prints her form on two-part no carbon required (NCR) paper.

Every few weeks, I send grade sheets home with a line or two about any big projects coming up. I make as many telephone calls as I can about good and bad behavior and good and bad grades. This practice is time-consuming, but worth it. I sometimes write short notes for individual students to bring home if they have improved significantly. The most important rule for me is always to return parent phone calls on the day I get the message. Before I contact any parent, I review the student's grades. If I can bring a grade printout to a conference, I do. It helps to point out patterns, for instance that a child is doing all homework but failing all tests, or doing all minor assignments but skipping major projects. I also try to bring a sample of the student's work with me to discuss.

—*Victoria Yeomanson, English teacher*

Student Progress Report

Student: _____ Class: _____

Area of Concern:

_____ **Tardies:** Student has been tardy (   ) days this quarter. Being late negatively impacts the student's participation grade and an excess of 8 tardies will result in a "U" (unsatisfactory) in Citizenship. Subsequent tardies may result in a Dean's referral.

_____ **Absences:** Student has (   ) absences this semester. Students with more than 18 absences will lose credit for the class.

_____ **Academics:** Student has missed (   ) assignments this quarter. His/her current grade is a/an (   ).

_____ **Behavior:** Student has been disruptive in class. Continued disruption could result in a referral to the office.

_____ **Other:** _____

Teacher Comments:

_____

_____

Please sign this report and have your son/daughter return it to me. If you would like to contact me to discuss his/her progress, I can be reached at _____ from _____ until _____ or (e-mail) _____ .
I hope that, working together, we can help your child be successful!

_____   _____
Student   Date   Teacher   Date

_____
Parent/Guardian

Parent comments:

_____

_____

The New Teacher's Complete Sourcebook: Middle School   Scholastic Professional Books

Preparing for Open House

You may feel a little nervous as you gear up for Open House. You will be meeting parents for the first time, and they will be checking you out to see if you are professional and capable. Be prepared! If you are well organized, you will feel more comfortable, and your presentation will be more successful. Create a handout that contains a brief summary or outline of the course content. Make sure that your handout contains the following information: classroom rules, grading procedures, policy regarding late assignments, procedures for absences and obtaining make-up work, expectations for homework, your room number, school telephone number and e-mail address, and the times you are available to conference with students and parents.

Plan Your Presentation in Advance!

- Begin with a quotation or an appropriate cartoon to break the ice.

- Thank parents for coming and explain that tonight is not a time for individual conferences, but that you will be happy to schedule a conference with them for a later date. They may also indicate their desire for a conference on the sign-in sheet.

- Introduce yourself and briefly state your basic philosophy of teaching and learning and your expectations of students.

- Hold up and briefly discuss the textbook or other materials used for the course.

- Distribute handouts and highlight the main points.

- Give a few concrete examples of how parents can help at home.

- Point out important bulletin boards, student work that is displayed, assignment calendars, and any organizational systems that you use in your classroom.

- Leave time for questions.

Tips for Conducting a Successful Open House

1. Dress professionally. Smile and show how happy you are to see the parents.

2. Be wide awake and energetic (even if you have to nap beforehand).

3. Be welcoming, positive and confident. I begin by smiling and saying, "Welcome to the Positive Zone!" I add, "I know the real reason that you are here tonight—why you rushed home from work, ate dinner quickly, and gave up a relaxing night in front of the TV. I'm so sure that I know the reason that I'm going to tell you. You're here to check up on me!" (Pause, because they'll laugh.) "Good! I'm glad, because that's what you should be doing. You should know who's teaching your child. You should know what the classroom atmosphere is like. That way you can help your child if he or she complains about the teacher or the work or whatever! And you can picture what life is like for your son or daughter in my classroom."

4. I then go into a brief run-down of classroom procedures and activities. I tell parents how I teach, supervise, check work, praise, and touch base every day with each student, by name.

5. Be sure to display student work very prominently throughout the room.

—Patricia Revzin, English teacher

Invite parents into your room with a warm smile and professional appearance. ▷

More Great Ideas for Open House From Experienced Teachers

Open House is a great time to connect in a positive way with parents and students. As parents enter the room, I have them sign in and state whose parents they are. Next to the sign-in sheet, I provide envelopes containing a 3- by 5-inch card with the following statement: 'Please list three things that you would like to have your son or daughter accomplish in my class this year.' I have parents address the envelope to themselves and then fill out the 3- by 5-inch card. I give a brief presentation of my course expectations and class procedures, and then I invite parents to find their child's work, which is posted on the walls. I collect the envelopes and the cards when the parents leave the room. The information on the cards helps me to know what parents expect their son or daughter to learn in my class. During the week after Open House, I send thank-you notes to all parents who attended, using the envelopes that they addressed to themselves.

—Heidi Olive, social studies teacher

Plan what you want parents to know and how you want them to feel by the time they leave the Open House. Write out what you are going to say in advance. Use analogies, stories, and ideas to make your points. Explain what you expect from your students and how parents can help. Make yourself available to parents, but do not focus on individual students at Open House. Invite parents to call to schedule individual conferences.

—Robin West, middle school teacher

"I usually begin by giving parents a little information about myself and the way I run my program. I follow this with a little problem solving, asking the student and their parent(s) to work together to solve a problem similar to what the students have been working on in class. I invite parents to share their work with the group. This activity gives parents an idea of what we have been working on and allows students to show their understanding of the material. I warn students ahead of time what kinds of questions they can expect to see during Open House, giving them additional incentive to learn the material.**"**

—*Eric Johnson, math teacher*

"Try giving parents the same interest inventory that you had your students fill out during the first week of school. See if they can predict their son or daughter's preferences and interests. It is a fun activity that parents will enjoy, and it is a great way to encourage positive parent-student interaction. See a sample **Student Interest Inventory** on next page. (And make sure you give parents a survey with the same questions the students answered.)**"**

—*Tracy Spencer, English teacher*

Student Interest Inventory

How much do you really know about your child's interests? Try to answer these questions the way you think your child might have responded during the first week of school.

1. My best friend(s) is (are)

_____ .

2. I would like my room to be the color _____ .

3. In my spare time, I _____ .

4. I get embarrassed the most when _____ .

5. My favorite sport (to play) is _____ .

6. My favorite kind of music (or group) is _____ .

7. The person outside of my family who has influenced me the most is

_____ because _____ .

8. My favorite subject in school is _____ .

9. My least favorite subject in school is _____ .

10. The accomplishment that I am most proud of is _____ .

11. The television show I hate to miss is _____ .

12. The hobby I enjoy most is _____ .

13. If I could have anything in the world, it would be _____ .

14. My favorite teacher is _____ . Grade or Subject _____ .

15. I really get angry when _____ .

16. I **do** or **do not** feel liked by other students at school. (Circle one)

17. I would like my future career to be _____ .

The New Teacher's Complete Sourcebook: Middle School   Scholastic Professional Books

Student Interest Inventory (page 2)

18. My greatest disappointment was _____ .

19. I wish I were better at _____ .

20. My choice for a vacation place would be _____ .

21. The book I most recently read was _____ .

22. My favorite family occasion is _____ .

23. My favorite food is _____ .

24. The food I dislike the most is _____ .

25. I think I am good at _____ .

26. My most prized possession is _____ .

What's Your Score?

☼ If you score between 20 and 26, you are a "top-notch observer" and listen well to the likes and needs of your child.

☼ Scoring between 15 and 20 means you know quite a bit about your child, but could improve.

☼ Between 0 and 14 means you and your child might not be communicating as much as you should.

If you are unhappy with your score, it is not too late. Begin to discuss the items on the inventory and spend more time communicating about things that are important to you and your child. Perhaps have your son or daughter take the Interest Inventory about you!

Addressing Parents' Concerns

After teaching for a few years, you will begin to recognize common concerns (or complaints) from parents that, if addressed in advance, will prevent potential problems. Following are actual scenarios that have arisen for new teachers and suggestions on how to handle these situations professionally.

> *My child has a 52% in your class.*
> *In all of his other years of schooling,*
> *he has been a straight-A student.*
> *I don't understand what is happening.*

When a parent approached a new teacher at Open House with this question, she replied, "He must be overwhelmed. It's hard for some students to adjust to seventh grade." Her answer did not satisfy the parents. Responding to individual parent concerns at Open House is a big mistake. If you do, you may find that a parent will corner you and monopolize all of your time, and other parents will not have a chance to meet you. In addition, you may be unprepared to answer their concerns. The teacher might have said, "*I would really like to discuss your child's progress and grades, but I am unable to hold individual parent conferences tonight. Please check the box on the parent sign-in form that indicates you would like to schedule a conference, and I will telephone you tomorrow.*" Unfortunately, the new teacher did not say that, and the parent left the teacher's room on the night of Open House and headed straight for the nearest administrator to complain.

The following day, the new teacher and her administrator met to discuss the student's progress. Upon close examination of the student's grade report, the teacher realized that she had inadvertently included the student's pretest in the cumulative grade. The purpose of a pretest is to help inform a teacher's instructional planning and to provide a baseline to be compared with the posttest at the end of the semester or school year. Including the pretest was a mistake that was easily rectified.

Another discovery for the teacher came when she realized that one of the student's low grades (40%) was a result of not bringing in a brown paper bag to cover his textbook. The teacher had planned to show all of her students how to cover their textbooks in order to keep them in good condition throughout the school year. Although this student had not brought in a paper bag, he had covered his book at home with materials purchased from an office supply store. The teacher realized that it was not appropriate to penalize a student for not using a specific material to cover his text, so that grade was also removed from the student's average.

Finally, the teacher found that the student had not put his name on one of his assignments and had not received credit for it. The paper without a name was hanging on her bulletin board. The teacher did give the student credit for the paper, even though he had not followed directions. After these three simple adjustments were made, the student's grade was 89%. What a difference! The parents were happy when the teacher held a telephone conference with them later that afternoon and explained her grading practices and the changes that she had made. They also agreed to help their son be more responsible by putting the correct heading (including his name) on all assignments.

Make sure that your grading practices are fair and that you can justify how you assess student learning. (For more information and suggestions, see Chapter 6: "Measuring Student Achievement.") Keep representative samples of student work to show parents how their child is progressing in your class. Finally, if you make a mistake, admit it and make amends.

> *My son is involved in many extra-curricular activities, including private music lessons, playing in a soccer league, and being in the drama club. In addition, his father and I are divorced, so he lives alternating weeks with his father and with me. He simply cannot complete all of the homework that you require.*

Many students are up to their eyebrows with parental pressure to be successful in every aspect of their pre-adolescent lives. They may have numerous activities and scheduled events that leave very little time for relaxation, let alone homework. New teachers cannot cave in to parents' ultimatums, but they can be considerate of the demands on their students' time away from school. You may want to allow a few minutes during the end of the period for students to begin homework and for you to check student understanding. Consider assigning fewer problems, such as all of the even problems in math. That way, students will still have the practice, which promotes retention of the information and builds skill mastery, but won't be overwhelmed. Talk with your school administrator to see what his/her philosophy is regarding homework. If a student has six classes, and four of his teachers assign one hour of homework each, then the parent has a legitimate concern about homework overload. If you coordinate homework assignments with other teachers on your team, students will be able to complete their homework in a timely manner.

I thought my child was doing fine in your class until the report card came home. Why didn't I have any warning that he was failing your class?

The issue is very clear when parents are blindsided by a problem that has been ongoing for some time. Parents have a legitimate right to remain informed of their child's progress in school. Most school districts provide unsatisfactory notices to parents at the midpoint of the quarter. You would be wise to provide progress reports for ALL students midway through each grading period. Keep parents informed so they can intervene when necessary to get their child on the right track. If it happens that a student is doing well in your class up until the last two weeks of the grading period, then you still have the responsibility to inform parents of the drastic change in their child's performance. A quick telephone call is in order. If you forget to inform the parent at an opportune time, schedule a parent conference as soon as possible with the child and the parent. After all, the child must assume some responsibility for the sudden nose-dive in academic achievement. Together with the parents, seek to understand what has happened to cause the change in their child's progress. You do not have to change the grade, but you may want to consider how to assist this student in getting caught up or understanding your academic expectations.

When dealing with parents, maintain your professional demeanor, no matter how defensive you may feel. It is wise to invite the school counselor or administrator to attend parent conferences. If you teach on a team, all of the other teachers on your team should be present for the parent conference. There is safety in numbers, and you will feel less vulnerable if a parent becomes unreasonable.

CHAPTER 8

Resources for New Teachers

As you embark on your teaching career in a middle school, you will be surrounded by young adolescents all day long. One disadvantage to being a classroom teacher is that you may sometimes feel isolated from other adults in the educational community. You may see other teachers briefly in the staff lounge when you check your mailbox, but you will be so busy that you'll find little time for socializing during the course of the school day. Certainly, there will be times when you need to meet with other professionals to obtain materials or exchange information. There will also be other times when you don't *need* to talk with other educators, but you'll *want* to—because you feel as though you are on an island. When that happens, you must reach out to connect with your colleagues. Build a network of professional support in your school and your district, and you will benefit greatly throughout your teaching career.

Connecting with Colleagues

As a new teacher, you may not be aware of all of the resources available to you at your school. As soon as possible, familiarize yourself with the building and introduce yourself to members of the staff. Believe me, your colleagues can be an incredibly valuable resource. The following is a list of people who can be of great help to you in various capacities. Some school districts may have additional resource people available to offer assistance to new teachers.

○ **Principal:** The building principal serves as the instructional leader and as the manager of all the school resources. He or she may delegate some of the responsibilities for operating the school to the assistant principals. Make an appointment with the principal to find out what his or her vision for the school is and what is expected of you as a new teacher.

○ **Assistant Principal:** Usually, in a middle school, assistant principals are responsible for supervising and evaluating certain teachers in the building. In addition, they may be given other responsibilities, such as student discipline, curriculum, the master schedule, student activities, or facilities. If you need assistance in one of these key areas, find out which assistant principal handles that area.

○ **Dean of Students:** If you are fortunate, you will have a dean in your school who is responsible for handling serious discipline issues that impact the school. Get to know your dean! He or she will have good suggestions for dealing with student misbehavior before it gets out of hand. Remember, you are responsible for addressing classroom misbehavior, and the dean is there to support you.

○ **Department Coordinator/Chairperson:** This person is usually in charge of all departmental resources, such as textbooks, novels, lab equipment, and supplies. If there are special contests available for students, the DC is responsible for distributing this information to members of the department. The DC is a good person to check with if you need more information about what types of resources you might use to enhance your lesson plans.

○ **Team Leader:** If you teach in a team setting, you will obviously want to get to know your team leader. It is this person's job to schedule team meetings, solicit feedback from other team members for the newsletter, and make decisions concerning the educational needs of your students.

- ☼ **Learning/Reading Strategist:** Check to see if your school has a learning strategist available to assist you with instructional strategies to increase student achievement. They usually have constructive, practical ideas in the areas of test-taking skills, enhancing reading comprehension skills, note-taking, organizing information, effective vocabulary-building strategies, and more.

- ☼ **Educational Computer Strategist:** This is your on-site computer expert! The ECS is there to assist you with incorporating technology into the curriculum and can also help you utilize educational software available at your school site. BONUS: If you want to know more about grade-book software, this is the person to see!

- ☼ **Librarian:** Ask your school librarian what the procedure is for scheduling time in the library. As you plan your research projects, consult your librarian to find out what materials are available. Librarians can also help you structure time wisely when you schedule time in the library. It is easy for students to waste time if they do not have assistance or if they do not have checkpoints. Also, make a point to find out what the clean-up procedures are. Your librarian will greatly appreciate it when chairs are pushed in, trash is collected, and books are ready to be put away.

- ☼ **Counselors:** This team of professionals is there to assist you with concerns you may have regarding student behavior, grief, abuse, and other student issues. Counselors also handle scheduling concerns, career counseling, and may be key players with school-wide testing. If you need assistance coordinating a parent conference that involves all or most of the teachers on a student's schedule, contact the counselor's secretary.

- ☼ **Special Education Teacher Facilitator:** This individual can be a good source of ideas on how to modify lessons to meet the needs of special education students in your classroom. The Special Education Teacher Facilitator may also have special materials and equipment available for you to use (such as cassette recorders, word processors, or computers) if required by a student's Individual Educational Program.

- ☼ **English Language Learner Facilitator:** This person coordinates the educational program for English Language Learners in your building. The ELL facilitator can help you make curricular adaptations to enhance comprehension for English Language Learners.

✷ **Principal's Secretary:** If you have a particular question, and you do not know who to ask, the principal's secretary will probably prove indispensable. He or she always seems to have a wealth of knowledge and can direct you to the right person. In most schools, the principal's secretary takes care of issues concerning a substitute teacher and can provide you with any official CCSD form that you may need.

✷ **Graphic Artist:** Plan ahead so you can submit copy requests to the graphic artist with plenty of lead time. Ask the graphic artist how to fill out the job order and if there are any requirements for using these services (i.e., minimum number of copies, turnover time, or using pasted originals).

✷ **School Nurse and Health Aid:** Any health concerns you may have about a student should be directed to the school nurse or health aid, as they have access to resources that are unavailable to classroom teachers.

✷ **School Police and Campus Monitors:** Not all schools have them, but those that do have school security are very fortunate. These people are trained to deal with serious discipline issues, such as student violence, possession of weapons and drugs, or other criminal behaviors.

✷ **Custodian:** In most schools there is a head custodian who supervises the custodial staff. You'll definitely want to find out who cleans your classroom, and occasionally bring that person treats—especially if you have had a project day where glitter or other messy materials have been used.

Selecting a Mentor

One of the most valuable resources that a new teacher can cultivate is a mentorship with an experienced teacher. Research from educational literature reveals that the most effective mentoring relationships occur when the process is one of mutual selection. According to Rita Peterson, author of *The Mentor Teacher's Handbook*, the most effective mentors:

- welcome newcomers into the profession and take a personal interest in their career development and well being.

- want to share their knowledge, materials, skills, and experience with those they mentor.

- offer support, challenge, patience, and enthusiasm while they guide others to new levels of competence.

- are more expert in terms of knowledge but view themselves as equal to those they mentor.

Get to know your colleagues so you can look for an individual who might be a good mentor. If your administrator assigns another teacher to be your mentor, don't worry if you do not hit it off with that person. Again, mutual selection results in the most effective mentoring relationship. Just remember that there will be many colleagues in your school with whom you may have more in common, so look around until you find someone who can answer your questions about teaching and be a sounding board for your concerns.

Experienced colleagues can provide a wealth of information. ▶

Top Ten Books for New Middle-Level Teachers

There are so many wonderful resources out there for new teachers, but these ten books are my all-time favorites. I continue to read them, even now after many years of teaching. These books will provide you with a strong background of practical ideas to help you be effective and efficient.

1 *Active Learning: 101 Strategies to Teach Any Subject*, by Mel Silberman. Needham Heights, Massachusetts: Allyn and Bacon, 1996.

2 *Awakening Genius in the Classroom*, by Thomas Armstrong. Alexandria, Virginia: Association of Supervision and Curriculum Development, 1998.

3 *Brain-Based Learning*, by Eric Jensen. San Diego, California: The Brain Store, 2000.

4 *Classroom Teacher's Survival Guide: Practical Strategies, Management Techniques, and Reproducibles for New and Experienced Teachers*, by Ronald L. Partin. Upper Saddle River, NJ: Prentice Hall, 2000.

5 *Cooperative Discipline*, by Linda Albert. American Guidance Services, Inc., 1996.

6 *Cooperative Learning: Where Heart Meets Mind*, by Barrie Bennett, Carol Rolheiser-Bennet and Laurie Stevahn. Bothell, Washington: Professional Development Associates, 1991.

7 *Designing Brain-Compatible Learning*, by Terence Parry and Gayle Gregory. Arlington Heights, Virginia: SkyLight, 1998.

8 *The First Days of School: How to Be an Effective Teacher*, by Harry K. Wong and Rosemary Tripi Wong. Sunnyvale, California: Harry K. Wong Publications, 1998.

9   *How to Assess Authentic Learning*, by Kay Burke. Boston, MA: Allyn & Bacon, 1998.

10   *The Courage to Teach*, by Parker J. Palmer. San Francisco, CA: Jossey-Bass Publishers, 1997.

Favorite Internet Web Sites for Educators

Lesson Plans

- ASKERIC Lesson Plans—**http://ericir.syr.edu/Virtual/Lessons**

- Kodak Lesson Plans—**http://www.kodak.com/edu/lessonPlans**

- The Explorer (K–12 Math & Science Resources)—
  http://unite.ukans.edu

- The Music Educator Launch Site—**http://www.talentz.com**

- Franklin Institute Science Museum—**http://www.fi.edu**

- McRel Lesson Plans—
  http://www.mcrel.org/resources/links/lesson.asp

- K–12 Lesson Plans—
  http://teams.lacoe.edu/documentation/places/lessons.html

- Scholastic Inc.—**http://www.scholastic.com**

Resources for Beginning Teachers

- **http://www.teachersfirst.com**

- **http://ed.gov/pubs/FirstYear**

- **http://www.inspiringteachers.com**

Virtual Field Trips

- http://wwar.com/museums.html
- http://www.si.edu/
- http://www.nasm.si.edu/nasm/edu
- http://www.field-guides.com/

General Education

- http://thechalkboard.com
- http://www.classroom.net
- http://ericir.syr.edu

Resources

- U.S. Department of Education—**www.ed.gov**
- National Science Teachers Association—**www.nsta.org**
- National Council of Teachers of Mathematics—**www.nctm.org**
- National Geographic Society—**www.nationalgeographic.com**
- National Education Association—**www.nea.org**
- The JASON Project—**www.jasonproject.org**
- EarthWatch Weather on Demand—**www.earthwatch.com**
- Library of Congress—**www.lcweb.loc.gov**
- Discovery Channel School—**www.discoveryschool.com**
- NASA Quest—**www.quest.arc.nasa.gov**

Five Worthwhile Professional Development Opportunities

In addition to your colleagues, professional development books, and great Internet resources, you will have other opportunities to continue learning about effective teaching strategies. Attending national educational conferences will give you a chance to share your ideas and hear from other highly motivated teachers. Choose your conferences wisely, as they are sometimes expensive. Ask your principal if there is money in your school's budget to pay for your travel expenses and conference fees. If so, when you return from the conference, you will be expected to share the wisdom that you gained! But that's not a bad price for what you get out of it!

Of all the conferences that I have attended, the five listed here are my favorites. They are well worth the money, and I promise that you will want to return to your classroom and implement the wonderful ideas and strategies that you gain.

☼ Boulder Nuts and Bolts Symposium of Middle Level Education: A Focus on the Practical!

Held in Boulder, Colorado, this July conference is a must for all middle-level educators. Contact Walt and Jan Grebing, conference directors, at (303) 455-5337 or e-mail: **grebingjw@worldnet.att.net**, for more information.

☼ Teaching for Intelligence Conference

Presented by the National Urban Alliance and SkyLight Professional Development, this conference features leaders in education who shed light on the multiple pathways of learning for diverse student populations. For more information, call SkyLight Professional Development at (800) 348-4474, or visit their web site at **www.skylightedu.com**.

✷ A Framework for Understanding Poverty

This two-day workshop, presented by Dr. Ruby K. Payne, Ph.D., will change your thinking about what poverty is and how it affects learning in the classroom. Profound understanding awaits you with this fascinating presenter who has indeed "been there and done that." Contact the aha! Process, Inc. at (800) 424-9484, or visit Dr. Payne's website at www.ahaprocess.com for more information.

✷ Teaching with the Brain in Mind: Brain-Based Learning

Eric Jensen, author of *Brain-Based Learning*, presents the latest research on the brain and how children actually learn. You will receive successful tips and techniques on how to use current brain research to inform your instructional planning, plus you will learn practical strategies on how to improve student achievement. Call (800) 531-0082 for more information.

✷ ASCD's Classroom Leadership Conference

This conference is a must! Led by award-winning classroom teachers, these workshops offer classroom teaching ideas for every grade level and subject area. You will come away with a plethora of practical teaching strategies to implement in your classroom. For more information, contact the Association for Supervision and Curriculum Development at (703) 578-5400, or visit their web site at **www.ascd.org.**

Voices of New Teachers

from the
Clark County School District, Las Vegas, Nevada

February 2001

In some ways, we are all new teachers every time that we embark upon a new school year. We learn from our students that we must not be passive planners or get stuck in a rut, teaching the same things in the same ways. Working with beginning teachers for the past four years has taught me valuable lessons about the struggles that new teachers confront during their first year of teaching. Their common frustrations and concerns in their respective teaching assignments may shed light on potential trouble spots for you. I have included them in this book to help you realize that what you may experience is probably quite normal in the course of honing your management skills and making the transition from novice to veteran teacher.

I really wanted to know what stands out in the minds of beginning teachers with regard to their first year of teaching. So I asked 600 (!) new teachers, "What was the most valuable 'puzzle piece' you found in terms of helping you become effective during your first year of teaching?" Now, hear the "voices" of 27 of those new teachers, as they responded to this question at the midpoint of their first year of teaching in the Clark County School District.

Seeing the Big Picture

"Teaching content material is important, but it is only half the goal. The skills of processing material, placing it in context, and applying it are critical to a successful future. Inspiring a love of learning and teaching the skills needed for achievement must also be included in the overall goal."

—*Joyce O'Day*

Connecting With Students

"I find it important to create a connection with my students by learning something important about each of them as individuals. It is a form of trust. This connection is what I then use to channel chemistry knowledge to the students. There are still a few students with whom I have not established this connection, and it bothers me. However, I am not giving up. They just happen to be more of a challenge."

—*Gary Coates*

Implementing All Good Ideas

"Teaching is a combination of classroom management, learning experiences, and various strategies, including hands-on techniques to enhance comprehension and create an atmosphere of acceptance and positive attitudes. I am still putting all these puzzle pieces together—taking parts and tidbits from every teacher I talk to, every service available, and every piece of paper about teaching—and forming my own unique jigsaw puzzle."

—*Kathleen Kundanani*

Connecting With a Trusted Mentor

"The most important piece for me this year has been my mentor. I have the opportunity to team-teach with a social studies teacher in my school. She has been a tremendous help to me! I can go to her for advice any day or time. She is a 17-year veteran and always has a good answer. She is also someone I can go to just to vent! The fact that she is also open with me about her own problems with students is of tremendous help to me; it makes me feel more **normal**! It's important not to feel alone."

—*Lisa Zweber*

Meeting the Needs of Diverse Learners

The most important puzzle piece this year has been using a variety of teaching strategies in my classroom. Considering the diverse learners in my classroom and developing lessons that meet the needs of all my students has been a challenge. I have attended numerous workshops and have had many opportunities to gather useful materials and resources. Organizing these materials and attempting to implement the different strategies in my classroom hasn't always been easy. Some of the techniques have been successful, while other strategies have required that I make some minor adjustments in order to adapt them for my classroom. But I'm beginning to get a better sense of what will work, and how.

—Michael Jackson

Engaging Student Interest

Throughout this year my priority has been classroom management and student behavior. But I've finally learned that it is most important to engage the students in interesting and motivational lessons. That and following through with discipline consequences has greatly improved classroom behavior.

—Brandy Philgren

Managing Paperwork

Finding the piece that solves the puzzle of paper management has been my quest. Without this piece, the rush of paper through the hole in the dam was threatening to drown me. There are still leaks, but the situation is manageable. Binders sort student information, paperwork, memos, receipts, notes, scraps, parent contacts, etc. The beginning of my prep period each day is devoted to sorting and filing paperwork and noting dates in my planner. Also, I learned to grade all of one assignment in a set whenever possible and to use some sort of grading rubric.

—Kiara Wolf

Hope for New Beginnings

The most important thing about teaching this year is the knowledge that next August I get to start all over again. I will finally get the chance to correct my management mistakes. I was not strict in the beginning, and my students discovered quickly that I was soft and new to the game. They basically ran all over me, and I am just now starting to get control. When I begin again next year, I will not make the same mistake. I look forward to the rest of this year and to next year.

—Nora Griffith

Structure, Structure, Structure!

Every time I have had a problem in my classroom, it has been linked to lack of structure. On occasions I have tried to take shortcuts, and that always comes back to haunt me. Don't overlook when you're tired or frustrated, but always persevere. Stick to the plan every day. No skipping steps!

—Jennifer Hartman

Becoming Technology Savvy

The specific puzzle piece for me this year has been the piece labeled 'technology.' I have been concentrating on using the computer more with the students in research and writing. My plans include previewing material as 'hooks,' clips for clarification, and videos for wrap-up activities more often. Students of today's world are advanced in the area of technology, at least in comparison to people of my generation. Fitting this piece of puzzle into my overall plan is a step in the correction of a weaker area.

—Eileen Randall

Pacing Student Learning

Timing was most important to me this year. I have a tendency to spend too much time on one thing and end up not covering everything I want to. I also think I'm very effective in most areas, but timing always seems to mess me up. Since I started working on it, class goes much better. The use of graphic organizers has helped my timing and the students'. It also helps me focus on students' prior knowledge to determine what I can leave out because they already have that knowledge.

—*Lorene Tuttle*

Management is the Key

For me, the most important thing this year was implementing a consistent classroom management plan. I realized that a great classroom management system incorporates so much more than following a set of positive or negative consequences. It involves thoughtful and purposeful lesson planning, feedback in a timely manner, as well as the ability to be fair. If the lessons are engaging, and consequences are enforced, then management is there.

—*Cyndi Clevenger*

Reading Students' Cues

The students tell you what they need, or at least that they need additional help. I have the knowledge, and that's the easy part. Imparting that knowledge to the students, for me, is the fun part. The students tell you with their eyes, hands and body movements if they are with you or if you have lost them. Sensitivity to students and the reading of their "presence" is the key to keeping me on track. Sometimes I even say, "Okay, that didn't work," and I change the strategy immediately.

—*Claire Hart*

Trust + Rapport + Discipline + Planning = Learning

When students trust their teachers, they will be more willing to ask for help. With trust comes excellent rapport between student and teacher. When trust and rapport are present in a classroom, discipline is minimized. Once the class is running smoothly, learning can be maximized. One way to gain students' trust and establish rapport is by being very effective in the way that you plan. When your classroom and lessons are organized, students will be more eager to listen and pay attention to your daily lesson and, in turn, will retain more of the pertinent information.

—John Corbitt

Being Consistent Pays Off!

Teaching my students procedures and being firm and consistent is finally paying off. I'm finally to the point where I can feel free to start expanding and focusing my energy and using my skills to create really interesting lessons. As a new teacher—and a roving teacher—I had a hard time getting my students to adjust to new procedures (they had been with other teachers for five weeks) and to accept me since they had bonded with other teachers. Being firm and consistent is ultimately what works.

—Selinda M. Henderson

Flexibility is a Way of Life

The most specific puzzle piece that has reinforced my teaching this year is flexibility. Flexibility is required in the real world. Teach students that the most important aspect of making a mistake is what one makes of it. 'Mistakes are nothing more than a learning experience.' Flexibility fits in here because if you need to change your approach to learning, getting along, or self-generalizations, then it is right to think of a new approach.

—Elizabeth J. Martin

Keeping a Positive Outlook

As hard as it is at times, I always try to end each day with a deep breath and a recognition that tomorrow is a new day. There are 'good' teaching days, and 'not-so-good' teaching days. With any luck, the 'not-so-good' days are followed and outnumbered by the 'good' days.

—Jacie Delvin

Transition From High School to Middle School

Cooperative discipline proved to be my downfall this year. This is my first year in middle school after four years of teaching high school. All these busy bodies entered my room and didn't want to stop talking. In high school, the bell always muted their voices. Now I had to figure out a new plan, one that would incorporate the team that I work with. I had the opportunity to visit another middle school in our district and observe the way one of their teams worked. This was the piece that put it all together for my team and me. I learned that I have to let the students see the real rewards that come with behaving. The students must be able to sense the rewards before they started trying to earn them. There have been bumps along the way, but now I'm ready for a great start in a new year.

—*Stacey Warnick*

Every Minute Counts

Making sure that there is always something productive for my students to do has been of utmost importance to me in teaching this year. I cannot let there be any dead, down time. If I do, that's when things start to get crazy. But just giving busy work is not the solution. I want them to actually learn while they are in my class.

—*Cory Thompson*

Learning Really Can be Fun

I really strive to come up with a balanced mix of the 'sweet stuff' with the 'healthy stuff.' We have a lot of fun…learning! A sense of community has been established that really goes a long way, and I believe that it is a necessity for success. I continually remind myself that if I am not having a good time, then my students are not having a good time. Do not be afraid to laugh with your students, and then laugh a little more.

—*Shalee Wells*

Working With Students in Poverty

"The most important piece of information I have received this year is what I learned about working with students in poverty, from reading *A Framework for Working with Children and Adults in Poverty* by Dr. Ruby Payne. Being a first-year teacher, I have found this information absolutely amazing. Not only did I discover new information concerning students, but also wonderful insights about myself. Many situations that come up in my classroom are happening for a reason, and those reasons are legitimate."

—Allison Granito

Organize! Organize! Organize!

"The most important piece of the puzzle has been organization. Thorough organization has helped my students by establishing rote rules and consequences, standard classroom procedures, and a clear expectation of lessons and curriculum. Organization has assisted my ability to teach effectively, interact with parents, and eliminate stress. Many teachers at my school say that a clean desk is a sign of an insane mind! All I have to say to this is that it's very relaxing to come to school and have everything prepared and easy to find!"

—Tracy Altman

Plan Well and Persevere

"The first day of school this year was a daydream that quickly turned into a nightmare! My sixth-grade students were too scared to do anything 'wrong' and my 'meanest teacher alive' imitation seemed to work wonders on them. I was on top of the world. I was the best. I was queen of the world. Then, sixth period hit. And I mean hit! The eighth graders streamed into my room as if they were the brass section of a marching band. The teacher who had these students last year sent a sympathetic look my way and said, 'Good luck,' as she walked into her room and left me in the dust. I girded my loins, walked in and started my 'classroom rules and procedures' lecture. By the time my students were finished with me, I was a bedraggled, quivering lump of Jell-O®. Fortunately, I didn't give up, and the next day I was even stricter. With perseverance and some good lesson plans, I have survived—at least for now."

—Vickey Codella

R·E·S·P·E·C·T

The most important puzzle piece would be learning to respect and understand your students. When you do this, your students are more willing to listen to you and to the assigned work. In your classroom, mutual respect will go a long way between your students and you.

—*Melody Geck*

Procedures!

Without procedures in my classroom, I would be so frustrated! They have allowed me the freedom to teach as I like to teach, without the hassles of discipline or constantly restating what I have already said.

—*Matt McMurray*

Finding a Healthy Balance

I had to find a system for attendance, grading, and lesson planning that would fit into my planning time. I took so much work home. Free leisure time every day is important and valuable. I'm still making changes to lessen the load and am finding new ways to pursue my hobbies. My sanity is important for effective teaching. I now use 4-MAT lesson planning, computer grading programs, and seating charts for quick attendance.

—*Melinda M. Skinner*

Collaboration Makes Learning Meaningful

As a school librarian, the puzzle piece most important to my teaching this year is collaboration. Meeting the needs of individual students, classes, teachers, and other staff helps the library become a central part of the school and learning environment.

—*Jill Savage*

Remember, every teacher was a new teacher once. Being a new middle-school teacher can surely seem a bit daunting; those first days—and months—will have their share of highs and lows, miracles and mishaps. But like all 27 of these first-time middle school teachers who survived their first year and plan to continue teaching—*and are even looking forward to it*—you, too, can turn this new situation into one of the most important and rewarding experiences of your career. As I said earlier, teaching middle-level students is actually an opportunity to hone your classroom management skills and to sharpen your sense of humor. And the more organized and prepared you are, the more successful you and your students will be. I hope this book helps you accomplish that. As a middle-school teacher, you can make a positive difference in students' lives and find great satisfaction in your work.

Index

Notes